Painting Symphony
(Exotic Fiction in Verses)

Painting Symphony
(Exotic Fiction in Verses)

K. P. Shashidharan

Sterling Publishers (P) Ltd.
A-59, Okhla Industrial Area, Phase-II, New Delhi-110020.
Tel: 26387070, 26386209; Fax: 91-11-26383788
E-mail: mail@sterlingpublishers.com
www.sterlingpublishers.com

Painting Symphony
Exotic Fiction in Verses
© 2013, K. P. Shashidharan
ISBN 978 81 207 8404 8

All rights are reserved.
No part of this publication may be reproduced, stored in a retrieval system or transmitted, in any form or by any means, mechanical, photocopying, recording or otherwise, without prior written permission of the author.

Printed in India

Printed and Published by Sterling Publishers Pvt. Ltd., New Delhi-110 020.

PAINTING SYMPHONY
is dedicated to
The Little King of Our Sweet Home,
- AAKARSH – My Son
& the Creator of Our Sweet Home
- Nishi – My Wife
& those Who Love Poetry

Acknowledgements

Writing poetry is highly risky, like tightrope walking over the Niagara Waterfall!

Though the author undoubtedly derives excitement in pursuing his poetic adventure, what makes it worthwhile is the sheer joy and value that verses can offer to the readers who still believe in celebrating the magic of good verses.

I express my wholehearted thanks to Mr. Surinder Kumar Ghai, a towering personality in Indian Publishing industry and the Managing Director at Sterling Publishers (Pvt.) Ltd., and the competent team working under his guidance for publishing my books with impeccable quality and finesse.

My sincere gratitude goes to Dr. A. P. J. Abdul Kalam, former President of India, distinguished scientist, visionary and poet; Dr. H. N. Kaul, President of The Poetry Society (India), a renowned poet and writer; Mr. Nirmal Kanti Bhattachrjee, Director, K. K. Birla Foundation, an established literary critic and writer; and Dr. K. K. Banerjee, Director, Raja Ram Mohan Roy, Kolkata Library Foundation, scholar and connoisseur of poetry.

I express my heartfelt thanks to all my friends and well-wishers who have suggested modifications on the initial draft. I am fortunate to have the love and trust of all who have unwaveringly encouraged and motivated me at every stage for making this book happen.

THE STORY OF 'PAINTING SYMPHONY'
Exotic Fiction in Verses

WHY SHOULD PROFESSIONALS READ POETRY?

"When power leads man toward arrogance, poetry reminds him of his limitations".

John F. Kennedy

World over, poetry is increasingly being ignored, though verses have been the preferred medium since the beginning of the mankind to preserve the essence of human wisdom. John Coleman, author of *Passion & Purpose: Stories from the Best and Brightest Young Business Leaders* has recently written in the *Harvard Business Review* that "Business leaders live in multifaceted, dynamic environments. Their challenge is to take that chaos and make it meaningful and understandable. Reading and writing poetry can exercise that capacity, improving one's ability to better conceptualise the world and communicate it – through presentations or writing – to others." (John Coleman, "The Benefits of Poetry for Professionals", *Harvard Business Review*, November 2012).

He argued that poetry should be read by business professionals to "wrestle with and simplify complexity" of business problems. According to him, poetry writing and reading may not only help to "develop an acute sense of empathy", but also enhance creativity, add beauty, meaning and purpose of life. The relationship between business and poetry may be indirect, but poetry nudges business leaders to be empathetic to the environment, responsible to the community, coaxes them to think out of the box for solutions to challenging business problems and transform them as greater human beings.

"There are poems that have literally changed my life..."

Winner of TS Eliot Award, 2012:
Poet, *John Burnside*

The BBC has also recently released a video on intersection of poetry on business titled "Can legal and financial language ever be poetic?" In the show, Jenny Kitching, a poet and the legal secretary at Pett. & Co observes, "When anybody wants to express more effectively, you're forced down the route of poetry."

To maximise the indirect benefits of reading poetry for creative minded, who may not find enough time to refer to world literature, religion and philosophy, some of the greatest quotes from the world classics and thought-leaders over the years have been cited in *Painting Symphony* to enrich the reading experience. The idea is to induce joy, compassion, creativity, innovation, imagination, thought-provoking ideas and messages to help in transforming the readers. My endeavour is to produce a collector's book of delight that finds a place in every home library and, of course, in the known libraries of the world.

HOW DO YOU PAINT SYMPHONY?

"Painting is poetry that is seen rather than felt, and poetry is painting that is felt rather than seen."

Leonardo da Vinci

PAINTING SYMPHONY is uniquely created as an exotic fiction in verses. The verses weave a unique web of a fantasy world—a poetic Garden of Eden. Painters, musicians, poets, singers, ballet dancers join the other characters in the Opera of Life. The actors relish consuming the forbidden and non-forbidden fruits of life. The poetic landscape reflects different shades of human emotions—love, envy, lust, greed, lie, betrayal, treachery, corruption and crime. The fiction is honey-dipped in reality, striving to be ecstatic, philosophical and erotic at times, depending on the theme.

The story begins with a few brushstrokes of colours to the universal human emotions. The painter uses an unusual medium—the pristine canvas of the flowing watery bosom of the River of Time! When colours are poured on desires, they bloom into flowers, and flow in the waves of time, like surrealistic paintings of liquid dreams. Many a lyric of the heart gets choked in the throat unsung. The silence of melancholy outpours spontaneously and sporadically in music compositions.

The book portrays the best and the worst of human emotions, entering into the warring forces between the Good and the Evil in the flow of the River of Life in the River of Time. The idea is to entertain, enlighten and exhilarate the readers, taking for a joie de vivre on a roller-coaster ride to an esoteric world—a Shangri-La of Phantasms! While unravelling the storyline, the attempt is to touch the heart, stimulate the brain and in the process denude the consciousness for re-discovery.

The joy of living comes packaged with the agonies of life. Lyrics of living are orchestrated and choreographed. Music notes get tinged by deep tones of melancholy. Feelings are coloured in tragic beauteousness of the dilemma of existentialism. Verses are kept reader-friendly, identifiable and communicative with the readers, carving a niche in content, format, quality and presentation.

Painting Symphony is a garland of 54 Symphony Poems, sequentially flowing like a stream of thought. The volume comprises 3 separate Books of 18 poems each; well-knitted into one whole; reflecting the indelible impressions on love, life and joy of living. Imprints on the leaves of life are curry flavoured with wide variety of symbols, metaphors, similes, imageries and icons from science, religion, medicine, metaphysics, philosophy, psychoanalysis, neo-paganism, tarot cards and varied sources. The book revolves around hatching new ideas; triggering innovative thoughts to the expanding blue horizon of knowledge and sowing highbred seeds of messages of joy in the fertile mind. There are varieties of dishes in the menu for gourmet's delight.

THE STORY OF PAINTING SYMPHONY

Book-1: The River of Time

The master painter gets busy in pouring colours on the watery bosom. He captures a few droplets of rhapsody. In celebration of joy, he dives deep and dances like a dolphin, takes a bath in the Sun-lit warm water and goes for a catnap. Like a bolt from the blue, he gets a watery kick from TORRENT TERRIBLE and the story moves on...

Nobody knows where the flow comes from and where it goes but it carries life ahead. The Show continues in its complexity. The River of Life zigzags through tough terrains. When words become inadequate to express, emotions prefer painting symphonies, mix colours into music of the soul, sculpt figurines, compose music, choreograph and dance ballets. The search is likely to bump into the discovery of the God Particle dissolved in the being.

In the Symphony of Water and Fire, the life waters are threatened by the burnishing 'Oasis of Chaos'. There, the civilization refuses to resurrect from the ancient burial grounds. On the New-Year, a music troupe welcomes a new dawn. What does the night see there?

Amidst the chaos, we hear the Symphony of Love. We are invited to a Cocktail party and introduced to beautiful people including playboys and play girls and psychopaths enjoying in diverse ways. We find an entrepreneur going for ballooning for hunting fresh ideas over the historic pyramids and temples over the barren lands.

A father waits impatiently for the arrival of the Little King of the Sweet Home. In the Flow of Life, a Strange Thief gets caught for robbing the most precious thing in life and what happens then? The bay bridge once built by the lovers is getting demolished by the builders themselves. What is the reason? What does happen to life when it moves rule-bound? Smoking relationship ends in fire, reaching the court room. There the love loses its symphony.

Book 2: Champagne Party in the Milky Way

We enter the Shangri-La of Phantasms. We realise our greatest enemy is within us. The twin brothers kill each other in cold blood. What is the motif for the heinous crime? In the ballet of Night and Moon, the loved one does not survive in a night long intense love making!

Triangles, symbolising Holy Grail, seek help from a tantric. In the Seed Hungry Fields, Designer-Babies are produced. We visit a happy village of the cradle of babies! Where are their fathers and mothers?

We watch the Ballet of Life where the ballerina suffers till she breaks out the black magic spell. In the symphony of life, the ballerina finds herself neglected and longs to be the violin of her maestro.

We come across a neo-pagan assuming a magic name in a ritualistic ceremony and establishing his brand of paganism. What are his plans? The nude fire dancers climb up the hilltop to welcome summer. May Queen is sad when her playmate—Green Man—is killed by her maidens out of jealousy. What happens thereafter? After the erection of May Pole, why do the Red Men rush up into the Scottish jungle at midnight?

In the song of Mahamudra, the guru Tilopa does not find Naropa, an ideal loyal disciple who is ready for the song. Naropa confesses to his guru why he is not yet ready. We encounter bizarre relationship hassles; fight for survival when vital organs are being consumed by disease germs. Hope comes alive in the new research. Blood swimming marines get ready for an operation swim. Do they guard the City of Nine Gates?

People love the Visible God on earth and pray for his life. In the Kiss of Fire, fire becomes flower consuming the candle. Does fire light a new candle of life? The dormant energy Shakti is on a mission to find her consort. Can we help her and in the process experience the blossoming of thousand lotuses in enlightenment?

We are taken aboard in a Wormhole by the most famous physicist and cosmologist of our times, Mr. Stephen Hawking. True, he is not able to move physically, but he unleashes his brainpower, mind, and heart. Stephen invites Marilyn Monroe, the legendary Hollywood diva, for a champagne party with him in the Milky Way. How does the party go?

Book 3: Kalki's War Against the Antichrist

The story begins in the familiar terrain of the Holy Unholy Land, where corruption and innumerable crimes flourish. The land was once known for the rule of its legendary blind King and his blindfolded husband-worshipping Queen. In the land, there are incredibly enviable options to die!

The land was once blessed by a benign smile, a symbol of righteousness. The same smile is now used for lawful and unlawful trading. In the farmland, can the corpses of farmers, suspended on the trees safeguard their lost farmland?

LIE entertains JUDGE by stripteasing and she becomes a stranger to herself and gets deeply wounded in the end.

A father is quite perturbed about a crime that happened within his home. Who did commit the heinous crime when he was asleep with his wife?

In the land, fixing games is much more profitable than playing real googlies. The story of the greatest teacher who was poisoned to death for being the wisest is a reality in the real world even today.

The wolf man of Freud tells his story. We are then introduced to the patients of love turning into Wolf

Men and Wolf Women in society. Who are they? What has gone wrong in their lives?

The dimple on the earth's cheeks signals apocalypse. The Antichrist appears in different evil incarnations. In the apocalypse, the Earth splits into bottomless pits. Anacondas of Amazon are flown like kites in the sky by the fire tornados!

The sea monster, slumbering on the seabed, comes for revenge, when the Planet Earth takes a hiccup. The earth shows her discomfort to her uncaring children. The Baby of Hope is to be searched out from the heaps of debris.

In the market, the fruits of the Mind Trees are sold recklessly in attractive packaging. Those fruits may contain poison and kill the dreams of the credible innocent minds. Finally, a dead body of dangerous Idea-Worms is dumped into the bottom of the sea to be devoured by sharks. There is crying need for curing the bedridden human soul to come out of the ICU. The pilgrims rush for a holy dip in the holy waters. Are they prepared for a holy ablution? Have they kept the life waters holy? Saints launder the stained minds and return to the people who soiled them to wear afresh.

The distressed pray for salvation to Allah at Kaaba from the core of their heart. Allah is there with them to do what is right. In the ultimate war between the good and the evil, the Antichrist kidnaps the Sun. How does Kalki appear on the scene? What happens in the war? Who does win finally in the war between the good and the evil?

Enjoy reading—Painting Symphony!
Brushing your moments in the colours of ecstasy!
Composing the symphony of your dreams!
Enjoy reading!—'Amuse Le Lecture!'

Contents

Acknowledgements vi
The Story of 'Painting Symphony' vii

BOOK 1
THE RIVER OF TIME

1. A Few Droplets of Rhapsody	2
2. The River of Time	6
3. The Flow	12
4. The Symphony of Water and Fire	16
5. Painting Symphony	20
6. Where Civilization Slept	28
7. New Year Baby	32
8. The Show	36
9. The Valentine Symphony	40
10. The Flower of Life	44
11. The Bitten Apple	52
12. The Symphony of Love	59
13. Arrival of the Little King of the Sweet Home	65
14. The Strange Thief	74
15. Cocktail Party	78
16. Ballooning Ideas	89
17. Rediscovery	94
18. The Bay Bridge	96

BOOK 2
CHAMPAGNE PARTY IN THE MILKY WAY

19.	Warring for Love	102
20.	The Ballet of Night and Moon	106
21.	Lie Goes for Striptease	109
22.	Seed Hungry Fields	113
23.	Triangles in Love	117
24.	The Ballet of Life	121
25.	Magic Name	130
26.	Casting the Circle	134
27.	Fire Dance	137
28.	Not Yet Ready for the Song	142
29.	Encounter	155
30.	Is It Time Now?	158
31.	My Name is c-Myc	162
32.	Blood Swimming Marines	167
33.	Visible God	170
34.	Kiss of Fire	175
35.	Awakening the Serpent	177
36.	Champagne Party in the Milky Way	180

BOOK 3
KALKI'S WAR AGAINST THE ANTICHRIST

37.	Holy Unholy Land	210
38.	That Benign Smile	218
39.	Farm Land	221
40.	Now You Tell Me	223
41.	Tossing Game	233
42.	The Poisoned Teacher	241
43.	Of Wolf Men and Wolf Women	252
44.	A Dimple on the Earth's Cheek	279
45.	Anacondas in the Sky	282
46.	The Story of the Fury	287
47.	Baby of Hope	289
48.	The Holy Dip for Salvation	292
49.	Hunting Strategy	295
50.	Idea Chicks	298
51.	Mind Tree	300
52.	Worms of Ideas	303
53.	Allah, my Allah	306
54.	Kalki's War Against the Antichrist	313

BOOK - 1

The River of Time

1

A Few Droplets of Rhapsody

A few droplets of rhapsody
Flower into dreams...
Those dreams bloom into flowers...
And flow in the river...
The river pours colours over them
Those flowers spread virgin fragrance
In the morning zephyr!

The ripples in the river
Bloom into rainbow rivulets...
Flow flowers...
Red, green, blue, crimson,
Black, golden yellow, pink tinges
In the flow of the molecules of joy,
The river turns into a Shangri-La of phantasms
The River in Colombia –
River Rio Cano Cristales –
Runs away to the Seventh Heaven!
SPRING is at soaring spirits,
Exhibiting his magnum opera---

'RIVER PAINTINGS'---flowing floral paintings
Over the wobbling watery bosom
Slicing them into small bubbles of joy...
The River goes for belly dancing
Shimmering vibrations overpower her!

In the raining golden energy
She dances, winking at, and flirting with
The **Rising Yellow Sun in the East**!
SPRING swims around in glee
Dives deep doing rounds of dolphin-dancing
Before going for a cat's nap
On the flowery river bed
In the afternoon, after bathing,
In the sun-lit warm water!

There came **TORRENT** in the stream,
Like a bolt from the blue
Woke up – **SPRING**;
By a terrible watery-kick
While the master painter
Was lost in slumber;
"You, bum of a painter,
Why sleep slothful all alone
On my Cristales' bed, during a sunny afternoon;
Instead of painting a maiden nymph?
Why not Skype Ms Muse of Murmur,

She'll pose before you to paint; the 'Power of Muse'
Or call Ms Virgin Verse for portraying the 'Fragrance of Virginity';
Or invite Ms Rhyme Nymphomaniac to model for you
To paint her soft underbelly in red colour of desire—
'Soul of Lust';
Imbibing fully the rhapsody in the nuptial!
Forget not to listen to the silent symphony
Oozing out of your mate's wounded soul
Mollify the agony of the tainted virgin's
Emotionally coagulant heart
With empathy dipped in transcendental love!"

SPRING yawned, stretching on the watered-down bed;
"Didn't you hear **MR TORRENT TERRIBLE?**
What the full moon witnessed in the last midnight
When those three sexy damsels
Went for gathering white, virgin, orchid blooms
For their beloved; searching on the hillocks
They were gang-raped, and buried alive, naked
By sadistic maniacs like you
And dumped down, forsaken, in the outskirts of human culture
In the gargantuan, garbage-dumplings of the city
Underneath heavy, heaps of man's hollow egotism
Riding the serpent hood of ego.
And overruling idiosyncrasy!
Didn't you hear their frantic screams?

A few Reflections:

"You may shoot me with your words,
You may cut me with your eyes,
You may kill me with your hatefulness,
But still, like air, I'll rise

Does my sexiness upset you?
Does it come as a surprise
That I dance like I've got diamonds
At the meeting of my thighs?
Out of the huts of history's shame
I rise"

Still I Rise: Maya Angelou

"A poet's work is to name the unnameable, to point at frauds, to take sides, start arguments, shape the world, and stop it going to sleep."

Salman Rushdie

"Painting is a silent poetry, and poetry is painting that speaks."

Plutarch

"When I pronounce the word Future
the first syllable already belongs to the past.
When I pronounce the word Silence
I destroy it."

Wislawa Szymborska

2

The River of Time

At sundown,
Before the night descends,
Hovering on the dark wings, like a falcon;
Our moments, get inebriated in champagne,
Suspended, in a cabin of the ship on the cruise;
Over the bluish, greenish waters of the River Nile!

Sipping the effervescence of joy,
You posed me a riddle;
"We're in a ship, riding over the waves;
The waves somersaulting in the river,
The river flowing on the Earth;
The Earth rotating on her axis,
While revolving around the Sun:
Now, you tell me;
Is the Ship, or the river, or life, or the earth
Which is really in the Flow?"

I know, in this ship
Life sails so slow

Let me be true to myself
Freeing me of hypocrisy
Why do I cover up anymore?
The fertile emotions springing out of me
Why do I bobbitise the budding feelings for you?

The last traces of champagne,
On your lips taste so blissful!
Overflowing feelings get freezing,
In the chilled, unfilled moments,
Overhung in the river breeze,
Condensed angst free falls, often,
Tenderly in the sky of my mind,
Like the virgin, white snowflakes!

In this city of memories,
I was frantically in search of love:
I found you –
A blossoming Red Rose,
Waiting for the nascent breeze to come,
To inhale her un-smelt fragrance!
A fountain of elixir springs forth,
Away from the whirlpool of oblivion!

Let my soft pecks
On your red lips linger on...
Like a cockatoo's clinging

Beak-kiss to its mate...
A little cooing and the red tinge,
Of blushing remain...
Before bidding bye, bye;
And flying to the distant horizon!

Forget me not...
Forget not, these moments...
For, these moments create,
Bubbling pearls of joy in us.
These instants, taste intense bonding;
Of friendship unbound, between you and me!
Let us immortalise...
This sparkling exhilaration,
Transmitting currents in our being!

I whispered; "We're on the move
This globe is on the move
Let us catch the waves,
Of the leaping time;
But, remember:
Time is the Flow!
Time is in the Flow!
And we're in the Flow!
Let us absorb,
And breathe in
The perfume of ecstasy,
Before it is too late!

Let us drink these droplets of ecstasy
Mind you,
The River of Time
Waits for none!"

I became busy, thereafter,
Engrossed in reading
The most gripping scene
From the most puzzling book--
--A Psychoanalytical case study--
That's you, my first and last real woman in life!
Let me ask you now a counter riddle;
Is this journey called life
From the Entry Point to the Exit Point
A dream? Or a reality?
Or a dream in a reality show
Or a reality in a dream show?
Or merely a big bubble, growing big,
And we make it growing big,
Bigger, and still bigger...
Just to be burst into nothing?
Or is there; something beyond?
An unknown journey;
Beyond this journey?
I know, surely I know;
I repeat, in the words of
The Philosopher King, Socrates;
I know, that; I DON'T KNOW!

A few Reflections:

"Drink to me only with thine eyes,
I will pledge with mine;
Or leave a kiss but in the cup
And I'll not look for wine."
To Celia: *Ben Jonson*

"A Book of Verses underneath the Bough
A Jug of Wine, a Loaf of Bread – and Thou
Beside me singing in the Wilderness –
Oh, Wilderness were Paradise enow!"
The Rubaiyat of Omar Khayaam:
Edward Fitzgerald

"Grow old along with me!
The best is yet to be
The last of life, for which the first
was made"
Rabbi Ben Ezra: *Robert Browning*

"Love's not Time's fool, though rosy lips and cheeks
Within his bending sickle's compass come:
Love alters not with his brief hours and weeks,
But bears it out even to the edge of doom"
Sonnet 116: *Shakespeare*

"The symbolic language of the crucifixion is the death of the old paradigm; resurrection is a leap into a whole new way of thinking."
Deepak Chopra

"Love is an element which though physically unseen is as real as air or water. It is an acting, living, moving force...It moves in waves and currents like those of the ocean."
Prentice Mulford

"Whether humanity will consciously follow the Law of Love, I do not know. But that need not disturb me. The law will work just as the law of gravitation, whether we accept it or not."
Mahatma Gandhi

"All that we send into the lives of others comes back into our own."
Edwin Markham

"You are my Companion; You are my Best friend. You are my Beloved; I am in love with You. You are my honour; You are my decoration. Without You, I cannot survive, even for an instant."
Sri Guru Granth Sahib

"Man, the period of whose life is one hundred years, should practise Dharma (righteousness), Artha (Wealth) and Kama(love) at different times and in such a manner that they may harmonize together and not clash."
Kama Sutra: *Vatsyayana*

3

The Flow

Originating
In the cloudy cavern of the past
The flow cascades down...
Like a celestial cataract
It surges ahead...
Knowing not, where to go
Searching for the estuary
To discharge what it carries
In its pregnant womb
Into the Black Ocean Mouth
In the Woolly Future!

Not easy to reminisce
Where we plunged
Into its course
Might have been chronicled,
By our predecessors;
Probably those couples,
Continuously getting busy,
In planting their seeds
In its flowing waters,

Adding fresh lives into its torrents ...
Some swim, against the current,
In dissimilar strokes...
Sail crossways, sideways bamboozled,
Looking ahead,
For the budding green blades of grass,
Far beyond the banks
A few get drowned,
Dragged powerlessly in the vortex,
Between the points of Entry
And the points of Exit;
The normal bandwidth,
Of which is common knowledge:
Though difficult to predict,
The exact time place coordinates!

Mortal beings,
Vaporise--
Into elements in moments,
In its limitless, timeless, fathomless,
Space-less, busy, gush...
Something,
We believe as truth
May turn out to be half-truth,
Until it proves to be--
In the end –
Hanging topsy-turvy -

A Big Lie!
As we evolve,
We add dimensions,
To the dimensionless course,
Strive measuring and judging,
The ever growing quantum vacuum--
--the spectacle of the mirage,
That recedes in the horizon,
Of the ever expanding knowledge,
Of the unknown continuum,
Of the ceaseless, space-less, boundless
Big Black Hole!

Did we drop wisdom,
Down the stream,
Racing away, kidnapping knowledge?
Is it ever possible to swim,
Against the Flow of Time?
Isn't it as difficult as returning
To the womb, where we came from?
You, come with me, please,
Hurry up, baby; we've to flow in the flow,
And we flow and flow...
In the River of Time.......
We aren't out of time yet!

A few Reflections:

"*I saw Time flowing like a hundred yachts
That fly behind the day light, foxed with air
Or piercing, like the quince-bright, bitter slats
Of Sun gone thrusting under Harbour's hair.
So Time, the wave, enfolds me in its bed,
Or Time, the bony knife, it runs me through.*"

Out of Time: *Kenneth Slessor*

"*Put away all hindrances,
let your mind full of love pervade...
the whole wide world,
above, below, around and everywhere,
altogether continue to pervade with love filled thought,
abounding, sublime, beyond measure.*"

The Buddha

"*One kiss, my bonny sweetheart, I'm after a prize tonight,
But I shall be back with the yellow gold before the morning light;
Yet, if they press me sharply, and harry me through the day,
Then look for me by moonlight,
Watch for me by moonlight,
I'll come to thee by moonlight, though hell should bar the way.*"

The Highwayman: *Alfred Noyes*

"*What this power is I cannot say, all I know is that it exists.*"

Alexander Graham Bell

4

The Symphony of Water and Fire

"I've been waiting for you since ages
To quench my ever growing thirst
Flow into me –
Right into my gullet
I'll guzzle you down in chock-full
Yes, you –
The longest water body on the earth";
Said SAHARA to NILE!

"Might be you're the fiery thirst of the world --
The insatiable greed of man;
But, you can't swallow me;
Even if you're the accomplice of the Sun:
Remember, I'm the River 'Gihon -'
'Abbai', 'an-Nil al-Azraq'!
I'm the Flow of Life,
Coming from the Garden of Eden
I was there in the Genesis
My name, you can read - in the Hebrew Bible
Mind you, I'm not scared,
The wars between the elements –

Water versus Fire,
Fought frenziedly over the ages;
And not so new', said NILE!

The Blue Nile swims,
Out of her mother's womb --
The Lake Tana in Ethiopia,
Gushes through the burning gorges,
Curling up - into the parched,
Zigzagging, ravines,
Falling down at Tis Issat...

The muddy, brown White Nile,
Meets a greenish blue mate:
The White and the Blue River-Lovers intermingle
Flow into the other, beguiling,
And blending in love,
Figuring out jointly a new way of life;
Where the East meets the West;
The Arabs meet the Africans –
At Khartoum!

The blue and white water pythons
Flow hugging intertwiningly each other
Singing the paeans of union
Meanders as the mighty River Nile
Right through the hellhole of life
Into the desert wilderness!

2

The fight of the elements, glimmered red,
Reflecting on the dark goggles you wore that day,
Covering up your expression:
I love water-surfing over the pools
Of your lovely bluish fathomless eyes...
Sorry, I had to denude the eyes,
No contrivance should be there in between us
To peer through the sparkle
Radiating from those naked lakes!

In the symphony of water and fire
Nile gifted to Sahara - a symbol of their love --
The Eye of the Jewel –
The City of Thousand Minarets---
The City of Pyramids and Catacombs---
The City of Cairo
The ancient womb of civilization!

In the 'commerce of the soul'
I carried you in my arms
Like smiles of sun, swaying over the green leaves
In the scented air, my ears listened to your pink secrets
And what my lips mumbled in the air;
"Gift me -- you in you
A Seed of our love
To enliven - these bubbling moments
In our life'!

A few Reflections:

"He who has not praised the thirst
and drunk the water of the sands from a sallet
I trust him little in the commerce of the soul..."
        Anabasis: *Saint-John Perse*

"I don't just love you...I love you very much..."
        Love Story: Eric Segal

"Oh plunge me deep in love – put out
My senses, leave me deaf and blind,
Swept by the tempest of your love,
A taper in a rushing wind."
        I Am Not Yours: *Sara Teasdale;*

"Be the change that you wish to see in the world."
        Mahatma Gandhi

5

Painting Symphony

Let me portray the inexplicable
Pouring colours over the canvas
Brushing over those fast fading faces
Flashing oil on canvas over the feelings to dry up
Sketching emotions, performing opera on the face
Painting a symphony – The Beauty of Love!

Let me sculpt the lyrics
For the figurine
Etching imprints of sensation
Pulsating in the deep vales of my mind
Carved out by moving torrents
Wreaking havoc on the love-torn heart!

Let me capture those dream-horses
Galloping in frantic race in a video
Find verses for their liquid thoughts
Outpouring, like molten lava
Before condensing into a statuette!
Let me unleash, the uncontainable
Desires going on procession
Throbbing throats, slogan shouting

Leading ahead, holding red flags
Blazing the bits and pieces, getting muffled
Gather in an ensemble, clamouring for justice!
I'll strive to decipher the scripts of the intent
Sketching those piercing emotions stamped on blood!

Let me use an eleven-dimensional camcorder
To record the travails of life, decoding the libretto
Embossed on stones, abandoned by humanity
In the graveyards of time!
Let me chant a hymn for meditation
In tribute to thy munificence
And film a sonata, in praise of thy name
Composing a few music notes
For unheard tunes of euphoria!

Let me cinematograph the flowering dreams
Eluding the senses, like butterflies
Evading risky clutches of a child's curiosity
Dancing in the wind, like a ballerina
Teasing senses, far beyond the horizon of phrases
Before fading away that romantic ballet duet
Staged over the excited ocean waves
Dancing in the glittering shower
Of the golden rays of the setting sun
Presented on the suspended stage in the air
In the distant western horizon-theatre:

Let me choreograph that dance of love
Of Yin and Yang in the perfect circle of life
In the love symphony, when the lovers
Turn to pink to red to crimson in essence
In the fire of passion in harmony
Immersed in the solo concerto of the violin!

2

Let me now compose,
The music for the rapture,
Deluging the river of empathy:
Declaiming the rhymes,
For anthems of camaraderie,
And shape out a testimonial,
For the couples engaged in ballroom dancing,
Over the ocean waves,
Their love saga on a white marble mountain;
Enlivening nearly perfect-love-lives---
Bubbling lies of those fairy tales;
I'm blind, though!

I hear voices
Dissolved deep in me
I'm inept to construe
Their true meaning!
In thy mighty flow

The songs of sacrifice,
Sound mellifluous to ears:
But rarer to hear the soft melody;
I might be deaf though!

I enjoy wave-riding,
Taking danger by horns,
Of those mighty Tsunami- Rhinoceros,
Charging against human munificence!
I love diving deep
Into the eyes of jeopardy,
Skiing over the fiery crescents,
And caving along tough troughs to the fore
Of tumultuous thought streams
I'm crippled though!

When big boulders,
Roll down the cliffs,
Pushing life,
Into the black-holes of melancholy,
Who'll teach us?
De-bundling life into beautiful combos?
De-complicating obsessions into hobby-horses?
Fishing ideas in the high ocean currents,
Escaping---not gunned down by the marines,
And selling the catch in the market places,
To make both ends meet;
I am hypersensitive though!

But, I'm not,
The face or the smile:
I'm not,
My deaf, dumb, blind,
Crippled, helpless being---
The absence of attributes,
Of the human existence!

You'll find me,
Only if you're a serious seeker,
Behind the chimera,
That veils the real me!
I'm part of the sound,
That reverberates,
Echoes, and re-echoes,
In the vales of your mind,
And all over the Milky Way,
In you, in me, in them,
And everywhere;
Even beyond the spiralling galaxies!

I'm that single,
The original, virgin sound,
That created the 'Brahmanda' -
The egg of the Cosmos!
You can feel,
The imprints on the membrane,

Beyond the theory of strings,
And the theory of superstring,
I'm in the Matrix,
Shrouded in magic, mystery and monstrosity,
Mother of all the theories---
The M theory!

I'M OM--
The 'Invisible Soccer Ball'
Being played, kicked around in the cosmos
I'm the God Particle in you,
The spark that lights life,
The Maker of you,
Living in you!

Worship me, if you find me,
Even if you're an atheist,
A narcissist you're, loving only you,
You can discover the real you
And worship you for joy of living!

You may perceive,
You're like Ted Hughes' 'Crow'
Enormously endowed and empowered,
Thinking—you only own the globe,
Going on crowing and laughing,
While God goes on sleeping!

The day you fall on your own feet,
Buckling down, your knees,
Under own weight,
When you begin showing empathy to yourself,
Trembling in the weather-beaten,
Craggy monastery of own aged ruins,
Ablution of the soul may lead to Nirvana!

Meet me, then there surely in you,
Or meet you-- in me, it is the same,
Probing deep into the being:
See, I've dissolved me,
Inalienably in you;
Like the silent murmur---
Of the thin tinges of fast fading life,
That leaves you one day alone
That day may be initiating you,
Into another unknown journey!
You only must have initiated me,
To meditate on the Absolute
Offering divine flowers
To the altar of my heart!

A few Reflections:

"Thou hast made me endless, such is thy pleasure. This
frail vessel thou emptiest again and again, and fillest it
ever with fresh life"
       Gitanjali: *Rabindranath Tagore*

"Interpreting a recondite beauty and bliss
In colour's hieroglyphs of mystic sense,
It wrote the lines of a significant myth
Telling the greatness of spiritual dawns,
A brilliant code penned with the sky for page."
  A Message from the Unknown Immortal Light:
          Sri Aurobindo

"When the bright angel dominates, out comes a great work of art, a Michelangelo David or a Beethoven symphony."
         Madeleine L'Engle

6

Where Civilization Slept

In the city of Mark Antony and Cleopatra
The River Nile flows into the River of Life
And the River of Life flows into the River of Time;
Measuring, demarking, in vain ---
A beginning and an end,
To the eternal flow!

In the twilight,
Before night chases daylight out of sight,
SAHARA's face turns into bloodiest red;
Rage goes up in flames:
NILE shows SAHARA's
Angry face in the mirror;
Crisscrossing over Nile's
Quivering streaming currents!

On the banks of the water body;
In an 'Oasis of Chaos',
A music band - 'Blue Nile' played a new album -
'Marriage of the White Nile with the Blue Nile'

Welcoming the birth of a New-Year baby!
The Nubian teens danced in duo
Celebrating in the piece of music
Feelings outpoured: raw, bare and wild;
Lust played trumpets in solo!

The dancers' shoulders caved in,
Breasts shimmered in glee;
Waists swung, knees bending down,
Hands moved in rhythm;
Vibration sending undulating waves,
Titillated amorous hearts!

Pelvic muscles burnished in the fire
Rising libido, ad infinitum,
PASSION swung drum- beating hips
Upward, backward, left, right and forth,
Hip-hop, bop-tap, tango,
Jazz, pop, rap, disco, salsa
Mixing country folk in pop,
Rocked in blue, blending and fusing,
A new day was to break, out of the dark night
Signalling birth of a new music composition!

The vales of their belly,
Circled around the islands---

----the belly buttons became the cynosure;
Belly dancers ignited desires,
At the epicentre of the show,
Hearts exchanged cupid's arrows aplenty!
There appeared in darkness,
The drunken militia in black uniform,
Drunk with absolute macho power,
Bullets jumped out of them,
Probing deep into throbbing bellies,
Gang raped, gunned down people,
Ripped open in frenzy—love hungry hearts!

The bleeding bodies spun in pain
Spilling blood over the sands,
Drawing new abstract paintings,
Of broken-up human kismet
Where the civilization feared to resurrect,
From the ancient burial grounds!

Those solid and the broken lines –
Forming the i-Ching of sixty four hexagrams
Signifying Yin----
The passive, dark, absorbing feminine;
And Yang----
The invasive, male energy occupying Yin!
Didn't we hear then
Shakespeare's voice ricocheting?

In the dark night from somewhere
On the banks of the Nile;

"She (Cleopatra) will be buried by her Antony
No grave up on the earth shall chip in it."

A few Reflections:

"The truth is not always beautiful
"Nor beautiful words the truth."
Tao Te Ching: Lao Tzu

"A great sign appeared in the sky,
A woman clothed with the sun,
With the moon under her feet,
And on her head, a crown of twelve stars."
The Songs of Revelation

"I have haled my horse by the dove-moaning tree, I whistle
a note more sweet ...Peace to the dying who have not seen
this day! But tidings there are of my brother the poet: once
more he has written a song of great sweetness. And some
there are who have knowledge thereof..."
Anabasis: St. John Perse

7

New Year Baby

New Year Baby is born:
Lights up the golden chandelier,
Yonder in the eastern horizon,
Cascading smiles of energy,
Envelopes the world in gold dust!

Yesterday is buried beneath the dark night,
To make sure never to resurrect,
Keeping aside in the abyss of time!
The future eludes,
Cosseting, playing hide-and-seek,
Camouflaging, behind the mystery,
Making an unknown, new tomorrow!
Enlivening the moments that ride now,
Demarking the energy hoof-prints,
On the canvas of time;
Building stables for homing those horses
On the move; haven't we painted,
A pink-coloured face of destiny?
Aren't we still brushstroking

On the face of the future,
In rose, pink, green, brown and red,
In colours of love, life, sweat, toil and blood?

Saluting the energy-globe,
That lights this energy-hungry world.
Bite a big bite of the energy cake,
Warming up the hearts,
Condensing in chilled sorrow,
Let us cleanse the dust of pollution,
Baptising in the energy pool,
Escaping, not being sucked by
The energy-sucking addictive black holes!

Let us join lighting a few candles
Marching of hope in the silent procession
Swearing to care the fellow beings
As much as you want them to care you
Awakening out of the ashes of dead discontentment
Come, please to kiss on the face
Of the new moment of glory
Painting a beautiful golden dawn of glory
Engineering an equitable, honey-milk world
Defeating those forces of evil doers, who
Hammer on the chest of our Mother Earth!

Let us empower the powerless, hapless humanity
Lighting a divine lamp of love in the heart
Feeding the hungry, empty stomachs
Clothing the denuded, sheltering the street children
Wiping the last tear drops
From the sunken eyes of the downhearted
Lighting hopes of a joyful tomorrow in their hearts
Believing in us, absorbing the golden energy of strength
To paint life anew, creating a new world
Of peace and joy in the global village, that's ours!

A few Reflections:

"Ask, and it shall be given you; seek, and ye shall find; knock, and it shall be opened unto you: For every one that asketh receiveth; and he that seeketh findeth; and to him that knocketh it shall be opened."
The Bible: *Mathew* 7.7

"A good word is like a good tree whose root is firmly fixed and whose top is in the sky."
Al-Qur'an

"One sun rose on us today, kindled over our shores, peeking over the smokies, greeting the faces
of the Great Lakes, spreading a simple truth
across the Great Plains, then charging across the Rockies
One light, waking up rooftops, under each one, a story
Told by our silent gestures moving behind windows."
One Today: *Richard Blanco*

8

The Show

The Play had begun,
Even before we realised
The contrivance was gifted to us;
But, what show we show,
What channel we choose,
With whom we perform;
Mind it, the Maker -
Might keep watching!

Is this show called—living
Is nothing:
But:
Dying, in slow motion:
And Dying is nothing
But;
Living in fast forward?

If we desire so,
Can we fix our eyes?
Unwinding...and going slow...

Or if we covet to skip, a few scenes;
Can we try, going fast forward?
But, remember:
In this show---
Re-play is ruled out!

Have we got the remote?
If so, grab it to choose the channel
But, if not, how do we control the show?
Can't we rehearse?
Re-play... as best as we can?
But, we're made to know, repeatedly...
The show that began---and is, now, on...
Must be ending sharp on time!

Is this show real or a mirage?
Or a dream?
Is there a show, even beyond this show?
In this show,
Aren't we like Schrodinger's cat?
Entrapped in a mystery paradox
In a bizarre thought experiment
In life's quantum mechanics?
Can the cat of Schrodinger run alive
Out of the box of the experiment
Carrying its life from the created
Absurdity of the destined doom!

Will the cat be killed or kept alive?
Will it be dead and alive in sync?
It's a cat's life anyway, but why
The observers differ in their observations?
Doesn't it bother to the life of the Schrodinger's cat?
Does the cat know, when it will be poisoned by cyanide?
Aren't we ignoramus like the cat of Schrodinger
Enmeshed in a paradox box
Running in panic, hither thither, blindfolded
Searching an escape route
Knowing not the scientist
Who's going on experimenting on our lives?

Let me ask you, whoever you're
Why do you put us cats in this mouse trap?
Into the multiple, illusionary, circus
Inside a cage, enveloping judgment
Dreams shouldn't be allowed to collapse
Constructing, and deconstructing like on Tarot cards
In the spheres, moving spiralling around
In layers and layers of concentric circles
Whirlpooling into dreams within dreams!
In the designed assembly of desires
True, mirages get bombarded ceaselessly
Delusions after illusions, stumble over the senses
But remember, we've to nurture the tree of our dreams
Giving all care it needs, and pouring water of life everyday!

A few Reflections:

"When one sees eternity in things that pass away
And infinity in finite things, then one has pure knowledge."
　　　　　　　　　　　　　　　　Bhagavad Gita

"You are a child of the universe,
No less than the trees and the stars;
You have a right to be here.
And whether or not it is clear to you,
no doubt the universe is unfolding as it should."
　　　　Desiderata – Words for Life: *Max Ehrmann*

"There is something about a Martini
A tingle remarkably pleasant;
A yellow, a mellow Martini
I wish I had one at present.
There is something about a Martini,
Ere the dining and dancing begin,
And to tell you the truth,
It is not the vermouth—
I think that perhaps it's the gin."
　　　　A Drink With Something In It: *Ogden Nash*

"Sir, my concern is not whether God is on our side; my greatest concern is to be on God's side, for God is always right."
　　　　　　　　　　　　　　　Abraham Lincoln

"The best and most beautiful things in the world cannot be seen or even touched—they must be felt with the heart."
　　　　　　　　　　　　　　　　Helen Keller

9

The Valentine Symphony

Oh, are you my Valentine?
If not, why I hear the symphony of silence,
Orchestrating in my heart,
And playing those music strings,
In high and low pitches;
Squeaking and rumbling my emotions!

Oh, are you my Valentine?
If not, why do these emotions liquefy in tears?
Why do the rays of light
Draw rainbows over the tear-streams?
Why am I humming rhyme-less rhymes?
And singing these lyric-less lyrics?
Why am I in a thought-picnic eloping with you?

Oh, are you my Valentine?
If not, why does exuberance of animation,
Light array of luminescent lamps,
In the corridors surrounding,
The sanctum sanctorum of my mind,
Loop us, in a rare festoon of luminosity?

Why do I feel a vacuum in my being?
Even with my iPhone5, iPad,
iPod, Facebook and Twitter...
Why am I feeling so lonely?
Hearing a melodious tone
Blending our dreams?
You and I must be part of the same symphony,
And you must be truly my Valentine.

I should've searched you and found out before
To share the fruits of life together when it's just ripe
When the flower just bloomed to puberty
Spreading its un-smelt fragrance in the breeze
I am giving me to you, and all that I've to you, take care
Pour your heart out; fear not, I'm your friend:
Gaze me through my eyes; you'll find the glistening light
You've been seeking for years, far beyond the tunnel
Let me hold you tight
Peering through the windows
Of your mind to absorb the anguish in you
Reading those lyrics scripted in your eyes!

I can read those lines on your palm
Looking at the expression on your face
Everything's going to be perfectly fine-tuned

This melancholy will go vaporising into thin air
Confide in me; I'll be with you, till life holds on
To save you out of the imbroglio
Drinking the elixir of true friendship
Drawing energy from within and around
Re-scripting our destiny in the book of karmic verses
In the alphabets of genuine concern and care
We've created a paradise for us together
We'll beautify it, adding new thought-architecture
And should we ever lose our friendship at any cost?

A few Reflections:

"She walks in beauty, like the night
Of cloudless climes and starry skies,
And all that's best of dark and bright
Meets in her aspect and her eyes;
Thus mellowed to that tender light
Which heaven to gaudy day denies."
      She Walks in Beauty: *Lord Byron*

"It is well to give when asked,
but it is better to give unasked,
through understanding;
And to the open-handed the search for one
who shall receive is joy greater than giving."
      The Prophet: *Kahlil Gibran*

"With thee conversing I forget all time,
All seasons and their change, all please alike.
Sweet is the breath of morn, her rising sweet,
With charm of earliest birds; pleasant the sun"
Paradise Lost: *John Milton*

"Hold fast to dreams
For if dreams die
Life is a broken winged bird
That cannot fly
Hold fast to dreams
For when dreams go
Life is a barren field
Frozen with snow."
Dreams: *Langston Hughes*

"Friendship is a single soul dwelling in two bodies."
Aristotle

"Imagination rules the world."
Napoleon Bonaparte

10

The Flower of Life

The mystery of creation
Sleeps in 'The Egg of Life'
Let us search out that pink, shy Cosmic-Flamingo-Hen
Laying the golden egg; and then hiding the secret,
Scripting inside the Shree Yantra---
---In the Matrix of creation
In a complex, mysterious geometry!

You said; the Earth seems speaking;
Though, nobody seems listening to her woes!
Who's singing the Gospel of Love;
In the Garden of Eden at this hour of the midnight?
Aren't you crazy after the dream
To search for the energy circles---
---detouring the Earth's Seven Chakra locations?

You coaxed me to move all over the continents
Like a newly initiated neo-Pagan to prove:
I spotted the Rainbow Serpent,
Cascading through the mountain ranges of Oregon,

Crawling all over the Mount Shasta and Mount Rainier,
Overlooking the Lake of Washington at Seattle!
You said it is the mouth of the serpent,
Spewing out life-energy of the earth-'PRANA'
That's the First Chakra of the earth, we knew;
Witnessing a great upsurge through a geyser!

Searching for the earth's Second Chakra,
We reach the 'Island of the Sun';
In Lake Titicaca; I showed you;
The Plumed Serpent looping around,
The earth's energy circles,
Intermingling with the Rainbow Serpent;
Snaking all along the path towards life,
Crisscrossing the South Pacific Ocean;
And it emerges at Uluru-Kaka Tjuta,
In the Valley of the Winds--the Third Circle,
Connecting through the same umbilical cord!

You confessed to me;
Glastonbury is the home,
Of the Holy Grail of our Mother Divine!
There's the fusion of the Holy Grail
With the Phoenix of Aquarius
We were at the summit of the Chalice Hill--
--The Hill of the Holy Grail--
The Heart Chakra-of the Phoenix

Is beneath the hill;
Where the alchemy takes place!
Shaftesbury is the home,
Of the Sacred Spear of Purpose
The ancient fertility rites
Performed on magic weapons
The bleeding lance of the Grail Castle
Might continuously drip blood as in 'Wolfram'
Or it might be a single drop of blood as in 'Chretien'
Those who know Cabala
Can we bind the Grail with a wand
And spot the spotting of blood inside the Holy Grail?

The Rainbow Serpent,
And the Plumed Serpent crawl along,
Reaching the throat chakra,
At the Middle East—At Great Pyramid,
At Mount Sinai and at Mount of Olives;
Where the Earth sings the Gospel of Life,
At the sacred places of the humanity
At Jerusalem and at Mecca!

'The Third Eye' of the Earth is the Sixth Chakra
Is the location of its pituitary gland!
Shouldn't it join the seventh chakra
The pineal gland to open the third eye?
Enters there the Aeon of Aquarius;

The energy serpent,
Clambering up to Mount Kailas in Tibet---
The roof of the world
---The world's crown chakra!

You said;
Leonardo da Vinci had portrayed,
'The Flower of Life'---
And the sacred geometry
Of the Seed of Life!
Didn't I show you then,
'The Tree of Life'?

I was hungry but you went on feeding
A ripened 'Fruit of Life'!
We saw someone playing there,
With the 'Seed Ray' on the hyper-sphere
I want to ask you; can he distil—
The pure consciousness of the cosmos!

The mind saw
A wild-spider weaving the web
—The Matrix of all matter!
You were smart to explain,
The geometry of 'The Flower of Life',
Forming out of many hexagons—
—An expression of the Super hologram---

—A reflection of the whole;
Depicting space and time!

You showed me Leonardo da Vinci's
Platonic solids, sphere, torus:
And explicated his use of the golden ratio of phi!
We read, the creation began on the First Day –
Making 'The Vesica Piscis'!
In the Chalice Well of Glastonbury, England,
We found the Vesica Piscis intersecting,
Two circles to form the sacred geometry!

Created on the Second Day-
The Tripod of Life!
And on the Third Day—A Sphere!
Adding thereafter;
One sphere, each till the Sixth Day:
And, the Seventh Day saw---
----The Day of Rest—Shabbat!

The Spirit of the Creator,
Cruises on a ship,
Over the surface currents of the cosmic ocean,
Pythagoreans drew an abstract painting,
Of the geometry of the human eye!

You told me
'The Egg of Life' has seven circles,
They're shaped like a multi-cellular embryo,
In its first hour of creation,
Curling in the womb of the sacred feminine!
I enjoyed seeing
'The Fruit of Life'----
----A symbol of one million circles!
You drew a few lines to show,
'The tree of Life'---
The blueprint of the universe!

You confided in me:
'In the spiritual quantum envelope,
Shakti or Shri gets pregnant,
At the centre of the inverted triangular chamber,
At the central, red coloured point of fusion,
From where the life blood oozes
Spotting in the sacred hole—'Bindu'—
In the Shri Yantra, Shri opens up conceding
Her consort Shiva to be in her always!'

I made it clear; I'm a physicist, not a meta-physicist
But I had to agree with you;
'Let us describe the phenomenon
Cosmic consciousness,
Coupled with gravity,

Strong and weak forces
Uniting with electromagnetism
Triggering after the Big-Bang
Progressively multiplying growth
In the quantum - one..two..four..eight..sixteen...
Alike the growth of cells in the womb!

At the Eye of Ra -
The symbol that denotes,
The power of the Pharaoh,
Before the oldest symbol of the 'Flower of Life'
We stood spellbound;
Swearing in to help blooming
Beautiful flowers of life
In the sanctuaries of our Mother Earth!

A few Reflections:

"*Mother of Grace, the pass is difficult,*
Keen are these rocks, and the bewildered souls
Throng it like echoes, blindly shuddering through
Thy name, O Lord, each spirit's voice extols,
Whose peace abides in the dark avenue
Amidst the bitterness of things occult."
For Our Lady of the Rocks by Leonardo da Vinci'
          D. G. Rossetti

"And down the long beam stole the Holy Grail,
Rose-red with beatings in it, as if alive,
Till all the white walls of my cell were dyed
With rosy colours leaping on the wall;
And then the music faded, and the Grail
Past, and the beam decay'd, and from the walls
The rosy quivering died into the night."
> **The Holy Grail: Lord Alfred Tennyson**

"As students are well aware, the Sword of the Grail romances is a very elusive and perplexing feature. It takes upon itself various forms; it may be a broken sword, the re-welding of which is an essential condition of achieving the quest; it may be a 'presentation' sword, given to the hero on his arrival at the Grail castle, but a gift of dubious value, as it will break, either after the first blow, or in an unspecified peril, foreseen, however, by its original maker. Or it may be the sword with which John the Baptist was beheaded; or the sword of Judas Maccabeus, gifted with self-acting powers; or a mysterious sword as estranges ranges, which may be identified with the preceding weapon."
> **The Quest of the Holy Grail: J. J. Weston**

11

The Bitten Apple

Imbalanced, losing all the controls over me,
I slipped out of me that day;
I was floored, I knew,
I was falling in for the first time:
The pain of being bitten -
A badly, bitten red apple;
And partly being chewed up:
Reddened, bruises spread,
All over the psyche;
A divine ache deepened,
Flashing like lightning, in my heart!

Cupid sent scented bouquets,
In cornucopia;
In the heady cologne of those red flora
I was busy in sculpting your model
On the island garden
Enclosed in the sky, patented by me,
You enquired;
"Where is the border of our sky-island?"

Said I; "Infinity is the border
Of the human mind,
Like the big 'O' of the cosmic womb,
The emptiness - beyond the emptiness,
Signifies not something, but everything;
And at times, signifies nothing, at all;
Except the infinite, orgasmic delight!"

"Is this mind, a micro-model of the sky,
God has gifted to us,
For endless cosmic journey and sojourn?"
"Find them"; I said; "in the flower of your mind,
Travel the infinite distance, till desires steam off,
Towards the end of the mind-cosmos..."

You wanted to know the colour of the mind,
I guessed;
May be like the colour of the infinity;
I stand corrected,
Like the colour of pure innocence
Mind, if kept pure, you know,
May be sparkling like diamond,
Looking like white, starry, crystals,
Might be like translucent, liquid crystals
Transcendental, sparkling bubbles of time,
Pure icicles, white, pearly, watery droplets of love...
Or like billows drifting, aimlessly, riding over,

Feathery, bundles of white, cotton clouds...
I know one thing only; that I don't know!

You asked then; "Is infinity God?"
I replied ingenuously,
"I'll find out; when I fly finally into the infinity.
Look at me!
Let me see through your eyes...!"
You said; "You're mad."
"May be, I'm!" – The Bitten Apple!
You make me wild, like a wolf
And at times---make me His Master's Voice---
Though occasionally I spewed out my irritation
Like the German Shepherd 'Blackie Woolfie',
We keep at the farmhouse in the cage,
Barking hysterically to be let out
To join the ball game of life played outside!"
And, often you've shed tears
As if a tear dam had been detonated
Or land mine, crumbling down,
Bombarded continuously by explosives;
Or outbursting volcano, overflowing,
Molten lava of angry vituperations:
Is this psychosis, we call...LOVE?"

Sharing the throbbing hearts,
Of being badly bitten by love bugs,

We remained between two kindled wands,
Lion in the Tarot card is thoughtful,
Focussed within:
You said; "Let me give ME –
As gift to you,
Do you promise to take care,
ME, my Love?
I love you, and I'll be there for you
You've become part of me and mine!"

I asked; "But; I've a question for you;
Why do we fall in love?
Can't we get up from the fall?
And move on in life?"
You said; "May be it's good,
Learning to walk out of the fall,
And, re-learning the art,
Like the small baby's steps,
To fall in love again with me more intensely"!
"But remember, it's risky to stand up,
When you fall in love"; you cautioned me;
"Never try standing up and walking away
Out of love, once you fall,
Never ever you adventure that!"
I painted that whole night to express my feelings
Pouring ink, acrylic, oil, charcoal, pastel on the canvas;

Still sketching with pen, pencil, adding more sepia
   and soot
I knew I've to succumb to the power of love....

In the commerce of love, emotions are sold cheap,
Love is manufactured for convenience
Plunging the souls, in the coloured liquid chemicals
Marketing them, exhibiting in the bazaar!
We idolize in vain—a heavenly saga of propinquity
In the sun, in the moon
Rejoicing the feelings of the hearts
Beneath the star-studded sky-dome!
I knew you loved money more than bare-fanged lust
Which anyone could buy in the bazaar
The professionals are there
Buying, selling, outsourcing love at extra premium
And for you, every love is lust, in camouflage;
Though I argued the converse--
Every sign of lust is the intensity of love camouflaged;
The other side of the love-coin!

What sort of love is that we profess?
Aagapic love—begins from liking each other
Advancing to companionship, seeking intimacy
Grow in passion, enjoying lusty, erotic love
Sharing interests, thoughts, dreams of life
Not degenerating to maniac obsession,

Aggressively possessive, dependent and vindictive
Enjoying games-playing with shopping lists
Do we have selfless concerns, maturing to romanticism?
Committing to relationship, before consummating love?
Do we fall in love again and again,
Only with the person who deserves?
Did we crucifix our LOVE, hammering,
The last nails of suspicion on the cross of relationship
Cremating love in a coffin in the garden
Offering periodical bouquets
Of fresh chrysanthemums and orchids
On anniversaries to the ghosts of love
Lying worms-eaten in the wooden box?

A few Reflections:

*"Lovers don't finally meet somewhere.
They're in each other all along."*

Rumi

"Love one another and help others to rise to the higher levels, simply by pouring out love. Love is infectious and the greatest healing energy."

Sai Baba

*"Pour the unhappiness out
From your too bitter heart,
Which grieving will not sweeten.
Poison grows in this dark
It is in the water of tears
Its black blooms rise.
The magnificent cause of being
The imagination, the one reality
In this imagined world."*
     Another Weeping Woman: *Wallace Stevens*

"Unto Thee Lord, the Soul of Creation cried:
"For whom didst Thou create me, and who so fashioned me?
Feuds and fury, violence and the insolence of might have oppressed me;
None have I to protect me save Thee;
Command for me then the blessings of a settled, peaceful life."
     Ahunuvaiti Gatha; Yasna 29.1: *Zoroaster*

*"Watch your thoughts; they become words.
Watch your words; they become actions.
Watch your actions; they become habits.
Watch your character; it becomes your destiny."*
     Lao Tzu

12

The Symphony of Love

You stepped into my life –
'The Queen of Wands':
Chaste, forthright, and loving;
I remained - 'The King of Wands':
A statuette of truthfulness, vim and vigour!

The 'Ace of Cup' comes out of the cloud
There's fish in the water:
You and I;
Continue to fall in and out of love,
Composing and failing to compose,
The Symphony of Love together;
Reciting, re-playing and rehearsing,
The composition of the soul:
Its lyrics, rhyme, rhythm, beat, bass and tune,
Conversing in the language of love!
Who says to impose enslaving laws?
Why do we cause the ear-splitting clatter?
Disrupting harmony in our symphony?

Listen to the music
Of the Song of the Soul –
The 'Suit of Swords' is with us,
We've double edged blades of thought
Remember, there's an eagle,
In the life's picture always
We should fight with passion,
For the desired end in mind
But shelter the chest
Holding two swords across
Away from the heart
Lest getting pierced through
By own weapons of destruction!
Hey babe! Shouldn't we come out
Of the crisis, like the King of Swords
And the Queen of Swords?

2

The music flows out of the flute
Along the rivulet of love in waves
Originating from the God-King of love
Ha, I can see, God's now on the banks
Of the River of Love, enjoying diving into the water
And swimming with the cow-herd maidens
He's Lord Krishna, the charming King of infinite love
Lost in the celestial symphony

Playing the music notes of passion
Over the heart beats of the maidens!
They dance in the melody brook,
Bathing nude, in bliss longing for him
Devouring the nectar of pure ecstasy
Playing on and on the strings of their hearts
--the soul healing life-hymn,
Leaving no notes of dissonance,
Healing the bleeding scratches,
Scrawled on the walls of awareness!

Let us swear to experience sublime love
More than we ever cherished,
For, living in love is life-replete
It is true bliss,
And true bliss is divine
Divinity is the God's prime attribute
And godly empathy
Is the soul of the love symphony!
Whether the Sun shines; or the Moon glows
Beneath the star-studded roof,
The divine love is experienced in the heart.
Light a sparkle of joy in the wounded soul,
Offer a flower of divine sparkle of life
To the love-torn hearts
Carry the divine spark of love to infinity
Let love dance in the circle of life

Immersing in perfect synchrony
In the harmony of blissful inflection!

I don't know, what made you to recite that day?
E. Y. Harburg's verse:
"Poems are made by fools like me,
But only God can make a tree;
And only God who makes the tree
Also makes the fools like me.
But only fools like me, you see,
Can make a God, who makes a tree."

I know, now you'll say, only a fool like me—paint;
The etchings of the heart, may be a fool like me
Can love a fool like you; come baby, let us compose;
The symphony that's throbbing in us!
You be the Queen of Pentacles,
And I'll become the Knight of Pentacles,
Riding on the horse to triumph,
Before crowning myself, as the King of Pentacles,
Haven't we got ten pentacles of mammon?

Oh, my dear, Queen of Pentacles;
I can read your horoscope, seeing,
The type of the element-shape of your face,
Those major zones of divisions,
Shape of your ears, eyebrows, eyes, nose, and mouth;
I need not listen to the sensuous lips' murmur

Might be camouflaging, what the heart conveys
I can guess your life possibilities, midlife crisis,
And of course the certainty of the final journey,
Packing off for the joyful journey to the alien mission
Carrying the hollow ego, packed tight, but hands empty!
Looking at your face, I can read clearly those lines
You've a sign of Aquarius in your birth chart;
Promise me, won't you nurture,
The Chinese Bamboo Fortune plants,
I got for you from Shanghai
And those Solomon Island's dark, green leaves
Of those herbaceous, fleshy money plants,
We've kept at home, while playing good and bad luck
Games of the Tarot-Cards- of our over-jumbled life!

A few Reflections:

"Restrain myself howe'er I try
I cannot stay unless I see
Beloved's face."
                                Risalo: *Sufi Saint Shah Abdul Latif*

"Without love a man stands alone,
separated from the core of existence,
without love everyone is a lone entity,
lacking any connection with others of his kind.
Today, man finds himself totally alone.
                                                            Osho

"Trusty, dusky, vivid, true,
With eyes of gold and bramble- due,
Steel true and blade straight
The great artificer made my mate."
                    My Wife: Robert Louis Stevenson

"A good wife is one who serves her husband in the morning like a mother does, loves him in the day like a sister does and pleases him like a prostitute in the night."
                                        Chanakya

"The will to win, the desire to succeed, the urge to reach your full potential… these are the keys that will unlock the door to personal excellence."
                                        Confucius

"Women and men have been and will always be equal in the sight of God."
                                        Bahaullah

"And God said unto Moses, "I am who I am."
              Exodus, Old Testament; "The Bible"

13

Arrival of the Little King of the Sweet Home

1

In those jubilant days of living
I was like 'The Fool'
Treading on the edge of a cliff:
Embarking on a perilous expedition!

Every night,
Meticulous was I to be at home,
To bequeath my ears,
Glued to your bosom,
Near the life pumping station
Over the heart chakra, waiting
It could be an obsession,
The fire in my soul,
Is consuming me from within:
A heart is in waiting, beating fast....
To listen to the rhythm of the beats of a new life---
----the music notes of a baby's heart:

Like a connoisseur of music,
Delving deep into a Mozart's symphony!

Before sleep went to bed,
In my droopy eyes,
One night I asked you;
'How did man get the idea
To gauge time?'
You gave me a smile,
Like a pink rose blushing in bloom;
"I guess; -- probably like you,
--a father of a baby,
Listening to the symphony of the heart
Of his baby in the mother's womb,
That Allah gifted to him!"

I want to be 'The Magician' then,
Possessing a magic wand of infinite power,
You were wise like 'The High Priestess',
Flying over the clouds of feminine insight,
Decoding sacred, secret, scripts of life's mystery!

Ears nudge again
Before 'Good Night' kissed your lips;
Before my eyes, urging me,
To move further down,
Traversing over the feminine contours;

Where nature hides, the mystery of creation;
Ears slipped, sliding down,
Over the bulging pregnancy curve,
Doing the job alternatively with absolute care
To eavesdrop---the sound of the music notes,
Of a life growing within you!

I hear drum beats
Clearly punctuated
By the tapping kicks
On the thin womb wall;
'I like you---'The Empress'
You're hearing the inner voice!
'An Emperor', I'm sitting beside you,
A proud father of a baby is waiting outside
The delicate belly wall of the mom of a child,
In between, in communiqué
With the replica of love, waiting inside!

Curious was I; "What shall we name
The fusion of our love?"
You asked; "How does man get the idea
What to name his child?"
"May be, listening to the baby
The father—speaking to –
The Child of the Father!"
"Call him"; you posed;

"Only if you prefer to"
"What?"; wonderstruck was I
You whispered;
"I mean the symbol of our love
Symbol of Allah's love –
Let me call him--NISHAN!"

I turned out to be 'The Hierophant'
Reading the inner psyche:
"I agree, we'll call our seed of love:
ICON – An Icon of attraction
AAKARSH---in Sanskrit"
"But, I've a nickname for him"
A secret, I share with only my offspring"
"Won't you tell me?
The special name of the child to his father?";
I pleaded.

"I'll call him"; you said;
"KICKY for fun,
Between you and me:
But, I've to ask the Prince
When he arrives!
You know, because,
I can't listen to the Little King,
As you do!
But, I want to remember,

Till I last,
Close to my heart,
His little patter kicks in me,
I'm a selfish mom of a little baby!
I won't share that joy with anybody!
Those baby kicks within me!"
We acted like 'The Lovers' locked in love!

2

Crying aloud, the mother at the hospital
Wriggled with pain,
Waiting for 'NISHAN' to arrive
Before the operation theatre;
You held back the pangs of labour
For a moment to say;
"Give me, a solid hug to survive
This growing birth pain in me!"

Clouds burst into lightning,
Pain was raining into tears,
'The Chariot' arrives
In the Sign of Cancer---
The raging bull is controlled
By stronger willpower
You presented me a memento
The fusion of our love!
The baby cried, being pushed out

Of his sweet home in you
The small world, cocooned by you
Inside you, taking every care of him
Possibly more than your life!

My eyes were lakes, inundated,
Tear drops formed tiny rivulets
Flowed out of those lakes,
Cascading down,
Through the black forest of my beard,
You're welcome---
The Little King of Our Sweet Home!

Holding the baby in my arms,
Thanking the Almighty
And you—his mom,
For having presented
The best gift of my life
Like Buddha,
'The Hermit' in me meditated;
'The Wheel of Fortune',
Will be moving ahead for sure
The blindfolded woman of justice,
Should deliver justice for sure!

Okay, you laugh at me; let me ask you, now?
Have you learnt how to read those Tarot Cards yet?

Aren't we sitting on a lotus in temperance?
Can you hear thunder in the clouds?
Lightning is glistening in the horizon
Is there burnishing fire
Behind the tall tower?
The moon swims out
Of the clouds-pool
Oh, yeah, there're pointed stars
Twinkling in the sky
Let us celebrate singing,
Dancing, giving and partying!

Hey, aren't we seeing the Sun in smiles?
While chanting mantras for our child?
Ha, ha! Who's showing?
That golden balance of judgement?
Can you see those beautiful hands?
Offering flowers for worship?
Hoh! I see a wreath, wrapped around the globe.
Earth is rolling down along the roads of time!
Amidst air... water... fire... ether... over and over.....

The Little King will take us ahead
Our genes, DNA and chromosomes
In the River of Life
Merging into the River of Time
Taking you and me

Into infinity in the eternal flow!
We love you, the Little King of Our Sweet Home
When you'll father a baby
Like your father,
Your father will remain antiquated,
Standing like a leaning tower of Pisa,
An Old Family Tree standing in pride
Showering blessings in abundance
For the unsurpassed best in your life!

A few Reflections:

*"Struggling in my father's hands
Striving against my swaddling-hands,
Bound and weary, I thought best
To sulk upon my mother's breast."*
      Infant Sorrow: *William Blake*

*"Your clear eye is the one absolutely beautiful thing
I want to fill it with colour and ducks,
The zoo of the new
Whose name you meditate –
April snowdrop, Indian pipe,
Little*

*Stalk without wrinkle,
Pool in which images,
Should be grand and classical*

*Not this troublous
Wriggling of hands, this dark
Ceiling without a star."*

The Child: *Sylvia Plath*

*"Our voices echo, magnifying your arrival. New Statue.
In a drafty museum, your nakedness
Shadows our safety. We stand round blankly as walls.*

*I'm no more your mother
Than the cloud that distils a mirror to reflect its own slow
Effacement at the winds' hand."*

Morning Song: *Sylvia Plath*

14

The Strange Thief

A strange thief arrived in her life
From somewhere
In one fine crack of dawn
He was weird
Because, he did nothing;
But fix his eyes at her engrossed.

When he knew,
She was well-heeled,
Having prized moments in life:
He began collecting
Those exquisite jiffies
And began living profligately,
Doing business of her emotions
Trading those pearly, jubilant instants!

Her eyes caught him,
While he was stealing from her
Those split seconds of bliss,
And trading them deviously

For making money in the fete
Those precious moments,
She had kept so far,
Locked safe
In the secret chamber of her heart!

She yelled at him transforming,
A conflagration in fury;
"You, bandit of a man,
How dare you rob away,
Those pricey gems of my life?
Return them right now!"

The merchant in him said;
"I don't have those gems
I traded them for cash!"
She insisted on him
To pay the right price for them
Or else he should return
Her pure heart of delight!

He pleaded innocence;
"I don't know their exact value
What I think all about is how to make money:
For me, they're gratis, that fetch good business
But, that doesn't matter, I can pay,
All that I have, for offering,

Those valuable moments in my life;
Only if, money could buy contentment;
Because, money meant nothing to me,
Except for trading in the souk;
But, I'm not guilty, because, you've already snatched
Those happy moments away from me
And now, both of us have lost them
In the murky mercantile wheeler-dealing!

A few Reflections:

"I have tried to write paradise
Do not move
Let the wind speak
that's paradise.

Let the Gods forgive what I
have made
Let those I love try to forgive
what I have made."
       Canto CXX: *Ezra Pound*

"Hope" is the thing with feathers—
That perches in the soul—
And sings the tune without the word—
And never stops—at all—"
 Hope' is the Thing with Feathers: *Emily Dickinson*

"Hold fast to dreams
For when dreams die
Life is a broken-winged bird
That cannot fly."

       Dreams: *Langston Hughes*

"We know less about the sexual life of little girls than of boys. But we need not feel ashamed of this distinction; after all, the sexual life of adult women is a 'dark continent' for psychology."
"No one who has seen a baby sinking back satiated from the breast and falling asleep with flushed cheeks and a blissful smile can escape the reflection that this picture persists as a prototype of the expression of sexual satisfaction in later life."

            Sigmund Freud

"Daddy, I have had to kill you,
You died before I had time—
Marble-heavy, a bag full of God,
Ghastly statue with one gray toe
Big as a Frisco seal"

        Daddy: *Sylvia Plath*

"Life isn't about finding yourself. Life is about creating yourself."

        George Bernard Shaw

15

Cocktail Party

1

In the city of the Huns—in Budapest
When the Danube flows,
Beneath the icy sheets of its skin:
Christmas parties warm up on its banks!
Spirits in hot 'Apple Punch' punch the hearts
Men GOOGLE in the eyes of women,
Search-engineering for a companion,
To warm up the bodies shivering beneath
The layers and layers of woollen costumes and lingerie!

Under the illuminated chandeliers of 'Palais Schonborn'
In Vienna, bottled oomph uncorks golden yellow
  cheers
A gentle hiss of freedom let go bubbling...
In effervescence of exuberance,
Golden giggles pouring down in the crystal cut glasses
Chilled by icy melting rocks, mixed with fuming
  passion
And honey, fruits, bitter!

2

Adult jokes join ballroom dancing, inhaling lungs full
Of cigar smoke, intermingling woody scents of the cologne
Cloud around the partying girls, painting their pointed pouts black
Busy tweeting, sweet little nothings!

Drunken eyes flip-flap, fly crisscross
Like butterflies, hunting for honeyed, colourful flowers
Merrymaking warms up in liquor,
Musings, music, gossip, and secret murmurs of hearts:
Their dreams erect many a Spanish Castle!

In the drunken, hazy, dusky air, guys go golfing,
In the early morning:
Dew drops on the green grass welcome them.
Delight illuminates their wide eyes, teeing off the ball,
In different putting greens!
Picking their match from the right group
And drive out in pairs for farther destinations!

A cool dude spots a group of 'Victoria-Secret' models
The guys flirt around chitchatting,
Ecstatic about their Milano bikini shows
Greenish eye shadows accentuate greenish blue eyes

Dreams mirror, rippling in the moonlit lake caught in desire
The curly blonde hair waves in a nod on an island of light
The beauty gets dripping wet on the Valentine's Day in agony
Punctures a few red-heart—balloons, smokes, boozes
Joins the guys to fornicate the night to heal in vain
The deep wounds of the love-ripped heart
What's there in commitment, relationship, love minus trust?
But burnishing the heart in hollow words of lie and deceit!

Ideas fly in the wild,
Some prefer going for swimming like sharks on a hunt
Holidaying in the bluish green waters
Of the Miami, Caribbean, blue lagoons
A long-legged brunette coaxes her jet-set billionaire boy friend
For a holiday to fly her to the 'God's own country' to sail on dream-boats
Over the backwaters; riding temple elephants,
Joining in bathing them in river, modelling, photographing
Laughing sitting on the tusk of tuskers and dancing amidst them
Knowing not the tamed elephant can be wild and risky at times

Becoming insane in musk, turning lusty uncontrolled
   after female elephants!

A few thoughts,
Get massaged for corporeal delight,
Amidst the long-legged cockatoos,
Agreeing to fly with those chaps,
For sun-bathing, water skiing, scuba-diving;
At the French Rivera,
Before joining the Monte Carlo,
Car Racing and gambling!

3

A wink of an eye rocks on the floor
Goes spinning in the fire of desire,
Sits on a pout of smoked lips,
Painted in purple orchid shade,
And whirlpools on her pink dimples,
On the cheeks of oomph for a while!

Passion ripens
Into a blood coloured mango fruit
Some painted mouths of design,
Get wet in red wine,
Look for smoky lips to get locked in;
To leave a bit of wine's red tinge,

Now only etching in rehearsal,
On the edge of the glasses!

The tall peahen tweets sweet nothings,
In the nose-pierced, gay guy's ear,
He goes for a laughing spree;
Swings in air like a palm tree in glee
Humming porn songs to please the cherry girl
Keenly in a long wait to her riposte,
To the hot, soft whisperings!

Air gets hot here in cocktail circuits
Even in the peak of the winter
Thoughts get stirred in flames
In the Irish coffee with liquor
Ripened passion harvests fruits to be consumed
Guys go gazing at chiselled feminine figurines!

A gay guy finds a **Fauvism** painting
'Le Reve', oil on canvas
Discovers swings in moods in **Picasso**
Meets a lady in pink,
Who winks at him, quoting **Picasso**;
"Art is a lie that makes us realise the truth!"

The man replies,
Citing **William Blake** in **Auguries of Innocence**:
"To see a world in a grain of sand

And a heaven in a wild flower
Hold infinity, in the palm of your hand
And eternity in an hour!"

She replies;
'If you like to capture the eternity
Come with me, the tick of my heart is a bit slow
Aren't you a cardiologist
Dealing with heart clocks?
Control the ticks of my heart machine
Make me believe, you're a damn smart,
Human-chronometer-repairer!
Time with me, walks at a snail's pace
Can't you check it and tell me, why is it so?
'Oh, yeah, I'm a heart specialist,
Also a fan of Einstein's theory of relativity!
The lady in pink joins him; and,
The two swans swim in the music-lake!

He orders a Duvet Platinum Passion
For her and whispers;
'I'm now a fan of you,
A cardiologist repairing your heart's needle
I'll sing an anthem in splendour of your beauty,
In this MOON-HONEY night of ours,
Blending our spirits in champagne,
With passion fruits,

Bonding us garnished with a white orchid!'
'But, Oh! Poor gay heart mechanic;
Why is your blood pressure soaring so high?
Didn't I engage you
To repair my heart going slow?'

4

An opera begins, now:
'You are in 'Château De Versailles' -
The Palace of Versailles –
Once the epicentre of power:
Trojan Aeneas play host to Dido -
The Queen of Carthage smiles,
The hero seduces the queen and forsakes her
Causes her dream to die
She sings -'Remember me'
It lingers on, haunting the soul;
But he doesn't hear!

Some sparkles of desire slip on the rim,
Oozing out, the juice of ebullience
Belly trinkets quiver in infatuation,
Curving seductively on a size zero waist,
Slipping loose, but clinging to the skin
Around the waist, below
The glittering snake of a gold chain!

An alpha male of the clan bends his body in flirting!
Dew drops of desire skyrocket in his mind!
Traverse it along,
The feminine voluptuousness!

A wild spider is let free, zigzags in the party arena,
Gets busy in a corner, begins weaving webs
All over the drunken eyes!
Eyes of a psychopath go crazy for a voyeuristic tour,
Snaking in, like wild creepers,
When damsels dance in the lush garden;
Peering underneath the leaves;
The covered curves and mounts,
Slinks sneakily, in lasciviousness!

It wasn't a solitary pin prick,
A momentary pain to let it go
But like a porcupine's poisoned quills
Deeply pricking deep into the consciousness,
Needling all over the tantalizing nerves' ends,
Where the fluid of ecstasy flows,
Leaving bloody scratches, bite marks,
Imprinting bleeding wounds on her psyche!
Bloody monster he is, burning in lecherousness,
She bids goodbye, escaping further crab-stings
On her sensuousness!
My iPhone vibrated in joy

Your voice cock-a-doodled a message;
'You know; what? I've booked a holiday with you
At Jukkasjarvi,
The world's best ice hotel in Sweden!
We'll celebrate our re-union, in an art suite!
You should come with me,
For the snowmobile excursions in the igloo villages,
We'll go for Tango, Salsa, Ballet,
I'll show you the fusion of ultimate brilliance,
Of Green and Blue Sheen,
There we're burning in flame!
Of the Northern Lights -Aurora Borealis –
The spectacular nature's show
And of course the human show is left to us
Winking at the green glimmering eyes
Of the North Pole,
The bluish, Reddish, Purplish sheen around
Doing Nature's romantic dance of patina!
I can't believe my ears! I've to kiss my iPhone,
And through it, I sent one hot kiss for you
And danced in the air - a peacock, spreading my wings
Singing through iPhone **E. E. Cummings;**
"**I Carry Your Heart with Me**":

"*I carry your heart with me (I carry it in*
my heart) I am never without it anywhere

I go you go, my dear, and whatever is done
by only me is your doing, my darling, I fear"
If you don't want to get hurt
Give your heart only
To those who can carry with care
Don't you ever give it to anyone!
Those who carry your heart, unauthorised,
However, might smuggle it through,
You're unaware, though;
But you can't be hurt anyway by those hooligans!

A few Reflections:

"The tree has entered my hands
The sap has ascended my arms
The tree has grown in my breast –
Downward,
The branches grow out of me, like arms
Tree you are,
Moss you are
You are violets with wind above them.
A child – so high – you are,
And all this is folly to the world."
                    A Girl: *Ezra Pound*

"You don't love someone for their looks, or their clothes, or for their fancy car, but because they sing a song only you can hear."
                    Oscar Wilde

"There are only two days that nothing can be done. One is called yesterday and the other tomorrow, so today is the right day to love, believe, do and mostly live."

Dalai Lama

"I did not direct my life. I didn't design it. I never made decisions. Things always came up and made them for me. That's what life is."

B. F. Skinner

"Your lips, O my spouse,
Drip as the honeycomb;
Honey and milk are under your tongue;
And the fragrance of your garments
Is like the fragrance of Lebanon."

The Beauty of Consummated Love: *Song of Solomon 4*

"You see things; and you say, 'why?' But I dream things that never were; and I say, 'why not?'"

George Bernard Shaw

"How gently and lovingly
you wake in my heart,
where in secret you dwell alone;
and in your sweet breathing,
filled with good and glory
how tenderly you swell my heart with love."

The Living Flame of Love: *Saint John of the Cross*

16

Ballooning Ideas

Afloat - in the sky,
Not in mind, like in kite flying:
I'm aboard - in a rainbow hot air balloon,
Over the banks of the Nile River,
Drifting over the desert land,
Hearing the roar of the dragon flame,
Gripping tight to the perimeter of the cane creel:
Intriguing is to see villages waking up...
When Karnack temple salutes the rising sun,
Colossi of Memnon rise from the crop fields
The balloon chariot sails across -
The sky over Ramesseum;
Near the Valley of the Queens!
Energised, when thoughts are stirred;
In the furnace of the mind:
When molten ideas blast and fume,
Eyes might go for grazing;
Like camels along the oases -
Not yet chewed up greens;
In spite of elephantine hunger of a desert!

Here, the history died in old age,
Sleeps under the pyramids;
Buried in classic style-
Beneath the gargantuan garden of remembrance!
Civilisation ran out of sight in fright,
Far away from those islands of cacophony;
And, corpses of times of yore lay relaxed -
On luxury bedstead in the necropolis!

I'm suspended, spellbound in a risky ride,
Clinching on the picnic basket;
Piloted by the tempestuous, blustery weather
Seeing the face of bereavement
Fuelled by gusto, in the air of resilience!
Mind goes for a jaunt
Reaching its ignition point
Then goes for combing its unruly hair
To attend the cocktail circuits
Far beyond the shifting horizon!

Ballooned Ideas
Mosey hither thither
In the limitless sky
In rainbow embellishment:
Fiery dust storm plays an orchestra
In the frightened psyche
Using a brand new music software!

When wind whistles tunes---
Thoughts fly boogie
In the wobbly terrains
Flapping wings like geese
Aligning in Victory formation
Stretching necks
Pointing only to the destination!

Piloting ideas
Isn't like a falcon on flight
Not just telescoping and micro-scoping
But zooming the eyes of granny knots
Bungee jumping into the smoking
Chimney of thoughts at times!

In a moment of mind vacuum
An air pocket might create a stir
Steering the balloon in hurly burly hubbub
What if, the undulating balloon sways away –
In a typhoon, bumping into other balloons
Ruptures, and if it is burst into flames
Thrown off those burnt bodies on the rocks
Along the banks, over the temples, sand dunes...
Desert vultures would hover around for carcass
There, the desert larks flock too
Camouflaging under the brown plumage
Calling in glee their mates

Desert eagles swoop on them
Though the Nubian bustards
Fail flying out of the Red-List of danger
What if, then, will those dead bodies come alive?
Like the legendary phoenix bird out of the ashes?

Mind turns tumultuous into a whirlpool
Transposing waves in progression:
It's good for the brain
To go for picnicking
In a hot air balloon
Steaming thoughts boost up brain buoyancy
Giving birth to seeds of ideas,
Researching resolutions to human quandary
Service to humanity can only illuminate life
What if, kite flying
Isn't an entrepreneurship?
Hot air ballooning is a free endeavour!

Is there a time for giving back what is due to the people?
Doing something really good
Giving back what we want to give to the humanity
May the pleasure of giving be ours!
To enjoy remembering what we enjoyed as beings
Humane to humanity, not like the hawk of Ted Hughes
Roosting in self-indulgence, in self-bloated glory;
Rehearsing, killing and eating!

A few Reflections:

*"I sit in the top of the wood, my eyes closed,
Inaction, no falsifying dream
Between my hooked head and hooked feet:
Or in sleep rehearse perfect kills and eat.*

*The convenience of the high trees!
The air's buoyancy and the sun's ray
Are of advantage to me;
And the earth's face upward for my inspection."*
                                Hawk Roosting: *Ted Hughes*

"Empires of the future are empires of the mind"
                                Winston Churchill

"The best way to predict future is to create it."
                                Peter Drucker

17

Rediscovery

Like a shooting star
Visiting the earth;
In a dash of a flash:
Sparks from your eyes
Bowled me out in flames!
I became then a victim
In your spider web,
While ploughing
Into the unploughed pastures;
And sowing seeds
Into the unexplored possibilities;
Mollycoddling only my selfish dreams!

I know now, life's ripples bury deep
In those fragranced memoirs:
Our dreams lost their wings
To fly together, to explore the secrets –
In the underbelly
Of the endless blue firmament
Desires go galloping into infinity -

Till the blood ceases to flow in the body,
And body ends into a box of dust -
Under the tombstone!

Now, I steer my life -
Towards a path of rediscovery;
Finding a new 'I' in me,
Unbundling the riddle that I'm;
Striving to work out
The fate I want to change
But, who's there to look after
My Achilles' heel?
Who's there to mirror me—
the reflection of my real?
And shadow me like a loyal friend?
It's time for me
To find a new 'I' in 'Me' -
By weaving a virgin web of imaginings
That might change the world for better!

A few Reflections:

"Oh, may your silhouette never dissolve on the beach;
may your eyelids never flutter into the empty distance
Don't leave me for a second, my dearest"
       Love Sonnet XLV: *Pablo Neruda*

18

The Bay Bridge

Her eyes gazed at him
For him, they played symphony in his heart
He was at sea, then
Searching for right expression
So he poured colours on the canvas
Settling down portraying
Paintings of the ocean of emotions
And ended up
In composing a symphony in colours -
Whose music notes
Only he played for her in camera!

Her blue eyes haunted him
Transmitting dancing waves of delight
Craving to join him
In his master orchestra, yet to begin
He loved playing with her delicate sentiments
Like a music maestro's fingers,
Dancing in dexterity on a piano keyboard
Bringing forth,
The rarest new high-pitched notes
Of ecstatic melodies!

A sea link was built by them
Between their hearts
Bridging the ocean bay,
Tumultuous in between their minds
Love began crisscrossing,
Dancing and singing over the bay bridge
Swinging titillated
In the sea breeze of emotions,
Being played in the orchestra
Of the harmony of hearts!

Time became terribly bored
And chained them in rules
Bridge began juddering
In life-quivering tempests
Storm develops in the lovers' eyes
Eyes of the storm focussed on blowing up
Rules bent and shook in the mighty whirlwind
The sea link cracked, not able to hold
Night saw the couple trembling on the bridge
Daylight saw them, red in vengeance
Hammering hard to demolish its steel pillars too
While life trucked over, limping and kneeling down,
Getting across, carrying the heavy burden!
Life created rattle and rage
In the thunderstorms, rain and lightning

Their hearts forgot the orchestra of love,
Not able to sing by them for years
Music of love deranged
Into terror roars of fury,
Chasing after them,
Like a tiger screeching in rage!

Babies' screams distressed
In the bellow, blast and blubber
Laws carried the broken pieces
Of 'bay bridge' on shoulders
Scampering to the court,
Where they brawled like cat and dog
The piano strings of the music maestro
Got rusted at the attic
Where spiders weaved cobwebs
For trapeze-dancing to prey
The torn, dusty canvas of colours
Lain curled up, discarded beside;
Love bunged up, crippled,
And not able to mosey any longer
In the court room, he saw
A pair of red eyes blistering in fire
He got ignited,
Becoming red fiery goblet of fire
Blasting and exploding
And finally emptying into nothing!

A few Reflections:

Whenever Beauty looks,
Love is also there;
Whenever beauty shows a rosy cheek
Love lights her fire from that flame.
When beauty dwells in the dark folds of night
Love comes and finds a heart entangled in tresses.
Beauty and Love are as body and soul.
Beauty is the mine. Love is the diamond."
                                    All Through Eternity: *Rumi*

"Love is not love,
Which alters when it alteration finds,
Of bends with the remover to remove.
Oh, not it is an ever-fixed mark
That looks on tempests ...and is never shaken."
                                    Sonnet CXVI: *Shakespeare*

BOOK 2

Champagne Party in the Milky Way

19

Warring for Love

The Sun-Leo
Enters into Libra
On the Winter Solstice
Splits into twins
'God of Light' and 'God of Night'!

On the day of the Autumnal Equinox
'God of Light' finds his alter ego
Peeking at him from the mirror
Growling like a lion, behind his shadow
Baring its claws, long razor-sharp fangs
Piercing deep into him
Blood spilling, bones crushing
Flesh tearing apart, saying;
'Sorry, I've to kill you, in cold blood
My twin brother
For the unpardonable crime
Of loving my virgin!'

The crime infects mind first
Rehearses many deeds of crime

Dreams of crime get enacted
God of Night enjoys living, loving Virgo
Erasing her memory with his twin brother
Making her his love interest
God of Night mates with the brother's love
And Virgo conceives a child
For him from his seed
To be given birth after nine months!

'**God of Night**' spots his dead twin brother---
'**God of Light**' oneday in the mirror
Hush-hush moving,
Behind him shadowing
Gawping at him in vengeance
In the offing for an opportunity to come
Waxing his muscles on the day of Vernal Equinox
He heard his alter ego murmuring;
"You are terribly busy with my love often
You ignore me brother, indulging deep in life
Don't you worry, you can't kite fly any more desires
I'm here, just behind you, shadowing very closely
And I'll surely catch you up in any moment!"
And his twin brother murders him
In cold blood in a split second
To cohabit with his love, Virgo
To indulge in love to beget an offspring
To be born after nine months!
The crime of murder is committed

In the game of selfish greed and lust
Brother kills brother, son kills father,
Wife kills husband, husband kills wife
The enemy is within, shadowing closely
Looking for an opportunity to eliminate!
The wars between the good and the evil
Between life and death, night and light
Go on endlessly, in cycles as long as life moves on!
Miss not, seeing beauty in the core of ugliness;
And ugliness at the centre of beauty;
Rejoicing the moments that life is worth for!

In the never-ending intrinsic dissonance,
Within the body, mind, and soul;
Will the evil win over the good,
On the day of the final judgement?
Will darkness swallow light?
When death chews off
The last bit of living
From the last cell, chromosome, and DNA
Should find the divine spark to cling on
Seeking out the 'Higgs Boson' in the being!
Let light walk alive, out of the shadows!
Let life walk out of the clutches of death!
In the final battles in the risky terrains of the very end
Let the glow that flickers continue lighting the soul!

You be the owner of that powerful dream
Possessing the power to wake up in the doom of destiny
Out of absolute darkness, glowing alive in light;
Waking up in an incredible magic of Alchemy
Walking out of the total black out of a coma!

A few Reflections:

"She gave him of that fair enticing fruit
With liberal hand. He scrupl'd not to eat,
Against his better knowledge, not deceived,
But fondly overcome with female charm."
          Paradise Lost: Book IX: *John Milton*

"At times wind from the burning
Would drift dark kites along
And riders on the carousel
Caught petals in midair.
That same hot wind
Blew open the skirts of girls
And the crowds were laughing
On that beautiful Warsaw Sunday."
          Campo de Fiori: *Czeslaw Milosz*

"An eye for an eye only ends up making the whole world blind."
          Mahatma Gandhi

20

The Ballet of Night and Moon

Light pours down in the full moon night
Forming a celestial stream unbound
Dipped in the wet fragrance
In the raining luminosity
Night blossoms into a smiling black flower
Dances like a ballerina in cool breeze!

Moon peers at **Night's** black face
Moon smiles bathing **Night** in divine love
Moon loves unveiling her dark attire
Night blossoms in wholesome black giggles
Darkness shies away hiding in black miasma!
Moon hugs **Night**
Celebrating the honeymoon
Kisses **Night** in her black mouth
Before going to bed embracing her closely
Moon buries his gleaming face
Between **Night's** big black bosom
Liquefying **Night** into light
In the ballet of love!

Full moon impregnates night
The seed of light is dark
Hidden in the womb of the New Moon
New moon grows to Full Moon
Full moon wanes to New Moon
New Moon waxes to Full Moon
Life celebrates the joy of light
Life celebrates the silence of night!
In the rivalry of love and greed
Crime is committed every night
Deviously, by design- in lots
Whatever is loved; kills the lover
As the thing of love contains the seed of enmity
Maker might destroy the creation
In satanic trance, killing might go on:
Father kills daughter, mother kills son, and vice versa,
What is perceived as reality might turn out to be unreal
Eyes might get blind, not able to see the reason
The wisest might turn to be a foolish monster!
The never ending chase after truth
Might end up in an endless dark burrow of time
Running like billy-o behind a non-existent shadow
Of a gargantuan meowing black cat
In the terrific silence of a new moon black night!

A few Reflections:

*"The wind blew east; we heard the roar
Of Ocean on his wintry shore,
And felt the strong pulse throbbing there
Beat with low rhythm our inland air."*

Snow-Bound: A Winter Idyll: *John Greenleaf Whittier*

*"Time will come
when, with elation
you will greet yourself arriving
at your own door, in your own mirror
and each will smile at the other's welcome"*

Love After Love: *Derek Walcott*

"Out on doorstep, morning is beating, beats on ocean's granite gateway and sun is sparkling near the world Half smoked gods of summer fumble in sea mist."

"In the Great Enigma", poem "Evening—Morning": *Tomas Transtromer*

"There is no other knowledge, no other learning, no other art, not even yoga or action that is not found in dance."

Natya Shastra: *Bharata*

"The heart of the person before you is a mirror. See there your own form."

Shinto Religion

21

Lie Goes for Striptease

Couching on a sofa at the Night Club
In the Champagne Room in ritzy light
The Judge of the beauty pageantry
Meditates on Champagne Night
Pouring smiles into the living moments
Waiting for the fashion show to begin!

Mind is scattered in diverse parts
Thoughts are in a marathon race
Stitching the pieces of mind together
Absorbing the wholesomeness in moments
The Judge empties the mind
Pushing out guilt in exhale, and;
Inhaling bubbles of joy
The judge sits in the secret inn
Wooing beauty in intercession
Unravelling the unbundled lies
Measuring beauty is a wild contest, here!

2

LIE catwalks on the ramp in fantasy wear
Showcasing silky fluffy outfits
Colourful nightgowns, swimsuits
Hide Me Not Thing-Wrapping Thongs
All trendy for the season
Beauties go for swimming,
Steaming and sauna, measuring,
Massaging and in water jets in Jacuzzi;
LIE wants to be the Beauty Queen!

The last of the show of beauty
Is the·Striptease Extravaganza
Stripping off the outfits that fit not
Feeling light in bikini like a feather
In the music of the rumba discotheque
Why shy? Has beauty got anything to hide?
Beauty moves, dances, gyrates in fun
Goes for gym, showing inside out
Doing acrobatics around the gymnastic pole
In an Amsterdam burlesque nightspot
The girlie show reaches its climax,
The final finer point of embarrassment
Unwrapping the wrapped purple cover up
The last bastion of the cynosure
Of the feminine, raw power of hollow flesh
The last cover up of **LIE** – her G-String slips off!

A beautiful gift indeed is body
Packaged in garments, adore it in gold
Naked or ornamented, painted or massaged in oil
Beauty has nothing to hide
But showcasing size zero brazenness!

Eyes sit all over the soft, bare skin
Poking and stinging like bees on flower pollen
The soft flowery petals of feminine charm
Befall red, blemished and wounded
Peeling off layers of feathery outfits
In fair, un-tanned, tantalizing skin,
LIE becomes stranger to her naked self
Seeing her reflection—nothing to hide
Scarred, gazing at her bizarre figure
She's looking like TRUTH?
Bleeding with poke marks all over
LIE now dives deep into the depth
Of the ripple-free transcendental waters
Hides herself, shying away coming out
To breathe afresh the Oxygen of life!

LIE feels frightened, denuded with no garments
Haunted by thoughts of guilt
For concealing TRUTH in colourful trendy attire
Mortified of exhibiting her nakedness!
Ablution in the celestial stream

Cleans off blots, splodge and blotches
LIE stands bare, self-conscious,
Aching in pain, white skin peels off,
Denuding herself for rediscovery
Waits for the final judgement
Before the Judge in meditation
At the Court of her consciousness
For the crime of fancy dressing and covering up
Credible, impetuous, innocent TRUTH!

A few Reflections:

"I was nice to him
He was nice to me
Only
Our doors, our window kept closed
Lest we smell each other."
                                                            Herta Muller

"Oh plunge me deep in love—put out
My senses, leave me deaf and blind,
Swept by the tempest of your love,
A taper in a rushing wind."
                              I Am Not Yours: ***Sarah Teasdale***

22

Seed Hungry Fields

Seed grows -
But - not in this field:
Because –
This field is crab eaten!

The field is changed:
But, still:
The seed sprouts not
The seed gets tested
It's worm-eaten!

Now,
A new field is leased out
New Seeds and eggs,
Are purchased:
A baby of five
Is born
In a borrowed vessel

Baby asks:
Who's my father?
Who's my mother?

Father and Mother wonder:
Haven't we got a child?

Hey lady, haven't I donated
A seed to the lab?
Hey, woman,
Did you donate or sell an egg?
Or buy my sperm?
Or lease your womb?
Or rent someone's womb?
Who's that lady?
Experimenting with my genes?

Aren't we mercenaries?
Selling paternity for buying a drink?
How many children do you want?
How may did you father?
Oh, my boy, tell me, by now?
The cryogenic laboratory-merchants,
Advertise my sperm
Hey guys, why is the price for a
Caucasian seed so high?
And African, Asian, Latino

Seeds are discriminated
Selling dead cheap, not many buyers, or what?
In the global human seed farming market
Tell me, now; by marketing my genes
And selling parenting dreams
How much gene-money did you profit?
My dear, well turned-out agent of a thief?

Owner of the leased vessel asks;
"You've to pay for my vessel charges, as contracted,
If not, my lawyer will speak to you
But how'll you pay
For the bleeding emotions of a mother?"
Will the cocktail of genes breed an idyllic offspring?
Out of eugenics, with no defect
In a utopian 'Republic' of Plato
To be groomed as the Philosopher King?
The Designer Baby Market
With zero-defects or not; knows not:
Who all fathered and mothered babies?
Fathers and mothers know not their children?
Blessed be the foster parents
And the Designer Babies
Coming out of Artificial Insemination!

Cloning we did, with frogs to begin,
Cloning we did; a baby sheep-Dolly, later,

Now, we go cloning--animals left and right;
Getting DNA, genes, chromosomes for test!
A wonder baby angel came out of a test tube –
Louise Brown, dear, wasn't she a medical marvel?
In-vitro fertilization is what we love to test---
Oh, yeah! Aren't we matching the eggs?
From the wombs of cows to human DNA
Aren't the stem-cells getting ready for human cloning?
To make a god out of man?
Aren't we doing the God's art?
Serving barren couples is godly indeed!
Let it be for any sex, for unlike gender,
For same sex, or for no sex or asexual absolutely,
Does this stuff, matter to God, anyway?
Is He going to be finally thrown out
Of his job by his ungrateful progeny?

A few Reflections:

"For if of these fallen petals
One to you seem fair,
Love will waft it till it settles
On your hair."

To My Wife: *Oscar Wilde*

23

Triangles in Love

Two triangles fell in love
Both wore the same symbol
Of the sacred mark of the Holy Grail
Their love begot nothing, but love
The triangles longed for a seed
Of love, out of their love!

They wooed a Tantric
The saint pronounced;
"Interpenetrating triangles
Conceive seeds of love!"

"But, how do we interpenetrate?
Aren't we inverted triangles?"
Tantric smiled and said;
"Pollination of the red flowers
Will be performed by a white flower:
Shall I be the chosen base triangle?
Blessed be you with fruits
In a divine tantric art of procreativity

In God's name under His holy decree
There will be union of three triangles
Footprints of a baby are on the way!"

2

In a town named 'Happy Village'
Amidst stray cattle, pigs and dogs
Saunter families of the poor
It's the Cradle of the World
Getting damn busy in making—human business!
Baby smiles are pasted on the walls
Amidst smells of sweat,
And dampened feelings in the clinic,
Bare footed, hungry women mumble,
Hanging around for leasing their wombs!
Come there, tender-coconut-sipping guys,
Gay couples, coming for buying wombs,
Surrogate mothers stand in silence in awe
Freezing their feelings in close silence
Money buys blood, cells, tissues, nutrients
Bulging bellies are fully exhibited in line
Lying in rows, exploited, subjecting for all tests!

The womb-clinic has the best wombs in the market,
Shows the bellies certified fit for growing babies,
Gay couples find fertile bellies certified fit,

Lease out the wombs in different deals
Doctors are prompt and right in advising
Lease out two or three wombs at a time
For, womb-renting is the cheapest here!
In our Happy Village, anyone can buy the best womb
We're the 'Cradle of Children'
Happily selling the best wombs for the least price!

Poverty sells human body, inhumanly,
And it rents out, sells out organs,
Aren't we getting the best tourist business?
Marketing the baby making machines dead cheap
Isn't it a win-win business to help the needy?
In the deal—I give you my womb, I win money,
In the deal—you pay money, you win a baby,
And we're leading in the womb selling business!
Might think of initial public offering and listing!

You know, I specialize in the business for lesbians
Marketing best man's seeds in the globe
Is my branded, new business, you can order on Facebook
My girlfriend is doing business for gay couple
Selling the best eggs of all shades of humans
Hah! Why do you need to love someone for a baby?
Love only for love, needlessly, why worry?
Why get into the unwarranted, baby syndrome?

The business of the womb is a billion dollar business
Making millions of babies all over the world
We freeze millions of eggs in cryogenic laboratory
Frozen are our sperms too, but not certified to mingle
Till you buy an egg! Buy a seed! Rent a womb
Let the egg meet the sperm, outside the womb
Put the embryo in a leased womb quietly humming a song
Grow a designer baby of zero defects, if possible,
Coming out of the ordinary womb on time for you!

A few Reflections:

"For oft, when on my couch I lie
In vacant or in pensive mood,
They flash upon that inward eye
Which is the bliss of solitude;
And then my heart with pleasure fills,
And dances with the daffodils."
>   **I Wandered Lonely As A Cloud:**
>   **William Wordsworth**

"Your nose, instead, through thick and thin,
remains between your eyes and chin,
not pasted on some other place—
be glad your nose is on your face!"
     Be Glad Your Nose is on Your Face: Jack Prelutsky

24

The Ballet of Life

1

In the ballet of life
Many a wicked magician
May cast black magic spell!
When the evil sorcerer
Seizes true love
Ballerinas may be cursed
To become swans
Swimming In the 'Tear Lake of Sorrow'
Formed out of the cloudbursts of emotions!

In 'Midsummer Night's Dream'
A white flower is hit by Cupid's arrow
It turns into purple in the magic
The juice of the flower,
Rubbed on the eyes
Makes the eyes to love
The person who comes before!

The fairies good and evil fight
And evil Caraboosse kills Princess Aurora
To be saved to sleep for hundred years
By the Fairy Lilac in 'The Sleeping Beauty';
The princess wakes up,
Kissed by her prince!

Clara meets the Nutcracker
The toy under the Christmas tree
Elopes with the toy, sleeps with him the whole night
A sweet dream, even though he's a toy man
The toy becomes the Prince in the magic of love
Here comes Nutcracker leading the Ginger-Bread-Soldiers
Defeats the Mouse King, in the war between good and evil
Wins the princess, dances in love for the rest of the life!

Black magic might cast wicked spell
Not for all times to come
The Black Swan will lose to the Queen Swan
The Queen Swan will win her Prince Charming
Love will win over wicked sorcery
And cast its magical spell!

The Prince swam in 'Swan Lake', mumbling;
"You're the dancing white swan

In my opera; come dancing, my ballerina
Do not swim any more in the swan lake
Join me in the ballet of my life
Let us fly, let us fly, fly far away
Out of the pool of pain, in the dusk
Breaking the black magic curse
Of the wicked magician
Let us share the apple pie of life
In camera in the full moon night!"

2

Toes bop; boogie and hop;
Bouncing, hoedown, skipping:
The fast moving feet,
Legs go dividing—wide open
Flying a feather in the air
Fever grabs the body in love
The whole body dances in trance!

Swans go easy in sensation
Feelings are caught in flame;
"I quiver on my feet, caress me,
If you don't, my whole body
Won't stop vibrating on my feet!"
Said the dancing Princess,
Looking at her Prince Charming

And her Prince responds;
"Let the opus be; 'The ode to joy' of Beethoven
Or let it be—'The four Seasons' of Vivaldi
Let concerto begin on piano
And later, let violin join the orchestration
Dance with me, you, my ballerina
Flying in the air, like wings on fire
Spinning, arching, curving in acrobatics
Lighting up, the lovely legs, stretching wide, in white flame
In the music storm, till the last breath, my danseuse!"

3

"An infant girl, I was, lost my home, my parents;
Used, overused, misused and abused;
Ran away—an orphan, in search of love;
Came to forget the sinners' faces
Lust played its composition so hard
The strings of my violin are broken,
Breaking down is my heart,
You're the maestro, came into my life,
Even before I bloomed into a full blown flower!

My life, I gifted to you, my maestro
You heal me in your melodious music
I'm your violin, abandoned at home
That music instrument is making painful notes

The strings are unused, resting, and breaking down
Play you, my genius—Bach, Vivaldi, Chopin
Play you, my whiz kid, Brahms, Haydn, Dvorak
Play you, my composer, Ives, Mozart, Beethoven,
On the music instrument that I'm
Play concerto on me—on my piano
Concerto on me---on my violin
Play Ave Maria on my cello now
Perform E major, e minor;
F major, f minor; D major, d minor;
C major, c minor; G major, g minor;
Allegro, Largo, Adagio, Presto,
Adagio, Largo, Allegro, Presto...

But you were obsessed often,
With those instruments, you loved;
I remained a silent violin, un-played;
Dazing to see you always playing with them!
You forget me, my absent-minded musician,
I'm still only your ballerina,
Dancing only on your tunes,
When will you come back to me?
Playing all major symphonies on me,
Playing all the 'Four Seasons' with me,
Taking out the music that choked in me;
Let my soul come out alive, again in an ode,
Let your artistic fingers run over me rhythmically

The nerve-nodes of your own instrument
Playing Sym... sym...symphonies...
Sym...sym...symphonies...
Allegro, Largo, Adagio, Presto...
Adagio, Largo, Allegro, Presto...

A concerto written in the key of D minor
A solo piano, flute, two oboes, two bassoons
Two horns, two trumpets, timpani and strings
Allegro, Allegro Assai, Adagio, Largo, Allegro, Presto
Take dark tonic key of D minor
Let the strings of my heart build a full forte
The piano of my body longs the movement
Tense me, stress me; let the timpani sound
Let tension heighten, stressing my strings
In the coda before the cadenza
Play me like a solo piano, that note of melody...
Lyrical...passionate...tender... romantic...
Sound that brings harmony and peace!

Let the composition end in me in crescendo
In an ascending light, in delicate movements
Ending in a faint whisper in the ears
Echoing, re-echoing in the valley of the mind
Let Mozart be played on the strings of my soul
Let this solo piano again ripple upward
Creating the Mannheim Rocket in eight notes

Let F major come in sharp piano chords
Snapping in bright melody in several modulations
Let cadenza brighten happy moments in the melody!

5

You're the Piano maestro, Violin maestro
My Chopin, Mozart, Bach and Brahms
Play on me the compositions, on me my piano
On me my violin, I'm that divine fruit
That's forbidden to the people, scared to enjoy
I promise you, I've kept the pentagram
Secure for you, deep down in me
Hidden in the depth of my hollow flesh
The secret of the mystery fruit
Brought down from the Garden of Eden –
'The Paradise Lost'!

Your journeying will finally lead you there
Seeking the mounts, curves, crevice of knowing me
The deep mystery of life hidden in me
The Holy Grail contains the seed--
--the Egg in the Flower, that makes life sustaining!
You might compose the best of the compositions ever made
Emotions are still stuck in the broken strings even now
Hey, maestro! How can it be true?

Are you a chimpanzee, yet to grow like a man?
Inexperienced you're in life; you hurt me
Digging your claw deep into the secret follicles
My soft pink petals are turning to blood red
You're insane—a monkey of a maestro
Manhandling femininity, you must know
Your type of fondness can kill me
Are you allergic to learning but music?
Learn the art and science of love making
From Kamasutra of Guru Vatsyayana
Enjoy display at Khajuraho and Konark temples
And grasp Masters and Johnson before touching me
And how to play me like a musical instrument!

Like a migratory bird, I've flown over
The seas, mountains to reach you
Seeking warmth in the distant land
A nest to lay eggs, a home for the chicks
You can sink into the depth of me,
But softly, searching your seed
I will encircle you around the axis
In the curvature of my hips!

I could be satiating you fully
The psycho of an instrumentalist
The thirst that dries in your throat
Might be quenched by the life-waters in me!

Your tongue has already tasted the pollen of the flower
Caress me, my maestro; I tremble on my feet,
My whole body gets vibration in the fever of passion
Let you forget your being in the composition of my love
May the best composition of music blossom
A Beethoven like symphony for the twenty first century
You shouldn't be perturbed by the humdrum hassles of life!

A few Reflections:

"Why do I love" You, Sir?
Because—
The Wind does not require the Grass
To answer—wherefore when He pass
She cannot keep Her place."
   Why Do I Love You, Sir: *Emily Dickinson*

"Yet half a beast is the great god Pan
To laugh as he sits by the river
Making a poet out of a man:
The true gods sigh for the cost and pain—
For the reed which grows nevermore again
As a reed with reeds in the river."
 A Musical Instrument: *Elizabeth Barrett Browning*

25

Magic Name

Sounds of gunshots in the midnight air
Shootings from AK-56 Kalashnikov assault rifle
Bullets rush into the bare chest of the dark night sky
On the night of the waxing moon, in a mad spree!

The man, who shot in the air
Gaped at the sky above
Adds up his birth date numbers
And throws away his weapon of destruction
It falls on the neo Pagan new Wicca deities
He doesn't care, for, they're his deities
He created his own order of Wicca
He dances naked in 'Octopus-Style'
Gulping a goblet of blood-wine
In trance, in ritualistic order, insane he was
A spinning psycho of a man!

Colossal was he in his birth robe
And commanded his head priest;
"I've chosen you my Hierophant

You're the Pope of my new Wicca order
I got tattooed my name on my waxed chest
Beneath the metal chain,
Below my Alchemy, spiral-goddess pendant
You must burn now incense
Over the purple letters—'OCTOPUS'—
That's my magic name,
You should know, now onwards!"

Beseeched his Hierophant;
"Octopus, shouldn't you cast the Circle first;
Summoning Air, Fire, Water,
Earth, and Spirit to bless you
Stand you, in front of the Spirit Candle
Facing the North; do write your magic name
On the paper in purple ink
Now, you've to burn it over in the red hot charcoal
I'll sprinkle frankincense granules in the fire
To consecrate your name in the smoke!"

A sky clad, fair female priest,
Tattooed and pierced all over her body
Came to the scene singing and dancing
Carrying a bottle of sacred herbal oil
She anointed the oil on Octopus' body
In the circle, before the spirit candle
At his wrists, heart and his third eye

Between the eyebrows, on his third eye
Then she marked a line,
Originating from the base circle upwards in oil
Linking all the seven energy circles
Over his massive body muscles
The Hierophant touched him then
With the pointed end of the sword
On the crown of Octopus,
The Hierophant spilled the blood
Drawing a line of blood there from
Moving down over till the base circle!
The Hierophant clanged the big bell
Hung on Octopus' hip; and Octopus danced
Dangling the bell, attached to him
Seven trumpets were sounded in the midnight air
The Hierophant blew aloud the conch-shell
And chanted the new hymn
Octopus ran amuck howling, jumping wildly in joy
Like a ferocious polar bear in the wild
Singing the new anthem
Created by him for his neo-paganism
The Hierophant chanted the mantras
And Octopus repeated;
'Blessed be me!
And my new name--Octopus!
May Goddess bless me!
By my new name!

I shall be known by my new name –
'Octopus' as long as live
I'll do whatever I like right for my order!"

A few Reflections:

*"A break in the circle dance of naked women,
dropped stitch between the hands
of the slender figure stretching too hard
to reach her joyful sisters,*

*Spirals of glee sails from the arms
of the tallest women. She pulls
the circle around with her fire.
What has she found that she doesn't
keep losing her torso
a green burning torch."*
      Matisse's Dance: *Natalie Safir*

"Any God I ever felt in church I brought in with me."
      The Colour Purple: *Alice Walker*

26

Casting the Circle

Cast the Circle;
But, wait for the Sun to sleep;
And the Night to change -
Into her darkest, black night gown -
On the New Moon!

The weaver's
Double spiral fire dance
Might be clinging to the waist
Of the Carlton Hill in Edinburgh
Clambering to the peak
Spiralling like a fiery serpent!
You stand—sky-clad;
You've nothing to hide
Gaze to the North
Take a pinch of salt
Mix it in the holy water
Bless, consecrate
The water and salt for the rites
Visualising the water

Exorcise of its energy
Sprinkle the salt water
Purify the place and the gathering!
Now, you drive
The energy in your Solar Plexus---
Let it go, let the energy flow, overwhelm you!
Let it go through your power arm!
Let it reach to the index finger!
Let the energy shower a fountain of light!

You've a white beam to weave---
Circles, horizontal, vertical, spherical around you,
Encompassing you
Blessed be you
Standing fully disrobed
At the centre of the energy sphere
Encircling a halo of power surrounding you;
"Soft of eye and light of touch
Speak ye little, listen much;
Decosil go by waxing moon,
Sing and dance like the Witches' [1]Rune;"

Light a yellow candle—for Air in the East
Light a red candle—for Fire in the South
Light a blue candle—for water in the west
Light a green candle—for Earth in the North

---
1. From 'The Alexandrian Book of Shadows'

Light a purple candle—for the Spirit at the Centre!
May you be blessed, invoke the elements
Meditate on your web, like a spider
Feeling fortified from the spiteful enemies
Immerse yourself in the inundation of liveliness
May energy flow through you!

You've cast the Circle of Power
A place for love, trust and truth to live—
A shield against the warring mischievous sprites
Transforming the physical to the ethereal
Creating a boundary between the world of men
And the realm of the divine Mighty Ones!
Now, you'll begin to hear—
The divine symphony of your soul!

A few Reflections:

"The air is dark, the night is sad,
I lie sleepless and I groan
Nobody cares when a man goes mad:
He is sorry, God is glad
Shadow changes into bone."

Refrain: *Allen Ginsberg*

27

Fire Dance

The fire dragon clambers up
Clinging to the waist of the mountain
Its mouth turns fiery red
Flickering tongue spews out fire
Casting a spell
Over the Carlton Hill in Edinburgh!

The sky clad fire worshippers
Beat drums, welcoming summer
Wearing only pendants
Ouroboros, alchemy armbands
Anklets, breast jewels, Horned God
Waist chains, pentagrams; ankh, solar cross
Gems of ruby, amethyst, emerald, sapphire
Spiral dancing in doubles,
The Pagans scale the hilltop!
The torchbearers show the forest pathway
The drummers beat passion to let it go wild
Performing ghostly pagan acrobatics
The wise Blue Men guide the procession

The nude, tattooed, painted feminine bodies
Guard their chest by the power of Pentagrams!

The Red Men show off –
Dancing on human pyramids:
The Red Women show off–
Mounting on the Red Men's pyramids;
Their Cowry-shells, tightly tucked in;
Secretly their underbelly!
The Horus Eyes ward off the evil forces
Emerges dancing and singing
The May Queen looks stunning
In rainbow butterfly fluffy costumes
Dressed like the fertile Mother Earth
Escorted by her White Warrior Handmaidens
The painted White Guards dance, shielding her
A moving tree dances around May Queen
Covered in lush green leaves is the Green Man!

2

The Pagans love dancing the whole night
Climbing up and down the hill in Scotland
The painted Red Men spin around, showing
The White Maidens; what they've got for them
The women spin around in fire, showing
The painted men; what they've got for them!

The show of the fire dancers begins at the Acropolis
De-bamboozles the mystery of fertility
Dancers bloom like fire-flowers
Enjoying, celebrating fertility,
Signalling the end of the winter
Invoking Air, Earth, Water, Sky, and Fire!
The Green Man escorts wooing the May Queen
Sharing Bannock Bread, washing face in the dew
The May Queen spins around, showing,
Her Green Man, what she's got for him!
While the Red Men tease the White Women;
The Green Man spins around, showing,
The May Queen, what he's got for her;
Green with envy, dancing wild in fire around
White Maidens kill the lusty Green Man
After stripping him off his bulky winter uniform!

The May Queen looks dejected
Missing her funny playboy mate—Green Man
The music becomes melancholic
Maidens dance around her in repentance
The love of the May Queen intensifies her sorrow
Enlivens the Green Man!

Drum beating goes insane
The fire dancers become exuberant
Music lights fiery vibrancy in the air
The fire dances around the fire dancers

The fiery red tongues of fire lick their nudity
Painting surrealistic dreams over the hills
Blazing passion goes crazy dancing in lust!

The Green Man dances, saluting the four elements
The May Queen crowns her Green Man, kisses him
Fire dancers dance around the bonfire
Losing themselves in the fire of passion
Dancing as if it is the last dance of their life
Fire dances over the hill around everyone in passion
Eccentric Pagans perform the best at midnight!
Erected down is the Maypole at Beltane
Piercing down into the depth of the fertile Earth
It is time for the Elements to unite in creative bliss
Red fire devils vanish in hurry, secretly into the Scottish jungle
Eloping with their lusty white fire maidens
To explore the mystery of fertility hidden in them
Before the Golden Sun peeps over the Carlton hill!

A few Reflections:

"Nothing in the world is ever completely wrong. Even a stopped clock is right twice a day."
"If I am part of your dream, you'll come back one day."

Paul Coelho

"On every full moon, rituals ... take place on hilltops, in open fields and in ordinary houses. Writers, teachers, nurses, computer programmers, artists, lawyers, poets, plumbers, and auto mechanics – women and men from many backgrounds come together to celebrate the mysteries of the Triple Goddess of the Dance of Life. The religion they practice is called Witchcraft."

Starhawk

"When the supreme reality is not understood, the study of the scriptures is useless, and study of the scriptures is useless when the supreme reality has been understood."

Adi Shankaracharya

"Dance as if this the last dance.
Dance with abandon, holding nothing back.
That will bring transformation to your being
and a possibility of transformation for other people too."

Osho

"Anyone who has lost track of time when using a computer knows the propensity to dream, the urge to make dreams come true and the tendency to miss lunch."

"Physicists analyse systems, Web scientists, however, can create the systems."

Time Berners-Lee

28

Not Yet Ready for the Song

In his 'Song of Mahamudra'
Tilopa sings:
'Mahamudra is beyond all words and symbols,
But for You, Naropa, earnest and loyal,
Must this be said:

The void needs no reliance,
Mahamudra rests on nought,
Without making an effort,
but remaining loose and natural,
one can break the yoke –
thus gaining liberation'
    (--Tilopa: "The Song of Mahamudra")

1

The body is a living sculpture
Ever changing architectural marvel
Carved out by the master sculptor
Modelled for the life forces

To flow through, like a flute
Outpouring the divine symphony!

Flowing afloat in the stream
Humming the tunes of celestial songs
I strived swaying like a hollow bamboo
In the blustery weather!
The choked arteries of energy
Might need cleansing
To smoothen the path
For the vital forces to gush through
The Song of Mahamudra
May unlock the knots!

Like a flautist
Let loveliness get-up-and-go
Passing through the sparkle that I'm
Seemingly playing through me
The Flute of Life
Brings the sweetest tune for my prayer!
Showering celestial cataract
From the heaven above
Cascades blessings, gushing through
It's the River of Love flowing
To quench the love-thirsty hearts
Healing the bleeding abrasions of living!

That phenomenon goes beyond my senses
Farther beyond the expression
An irresistible and overpowering feeling
Builds a golden bridge of empathy
Transmitting an orgasmic divine light
I want to be a baby in bliss in the cosmic womb!

2

Join me, dancing in the waves of love
Flow easy like water in the stream of love
The cool breeze in the morning
Carry the whiff of munificence to life everywhere
I want to be a seeker, lost in the search
I want to be a lover, being love, lost in the act of love
I like to be a singer, lost in the song
I prefer to be a musician, lost in the composition
I'm the worshipper, who became the prayer!

The music goes well
When the musician delves deep
Into the bottom of the ocean of the soul
Swimming smooth in the life waters of the tune!
In the sound of music,
When love composes its best composition,
The God stands knocking at the door of the heart,
Grinning in every sublime ray of thought!

Isn't it time for unbolting
The doors of heart
To let piety pass through
Lighting a torch of hope for the future?

3

"Do you listen to the song of your soul?
Have you become the music of the song?
Do you hear the chiming bells of the temple?
In the harmony of its melody,
Do your heartbeats dance rhythmically in ecstasy?
Experience the vibrations in you
Peaking in orgasmic elation at times
Being a human is nothing—but living in love
And be humane is better
Becoming an embodiment of benevolence!
You may urge to perform
 'Laithan' to begin with, to let loose your body
In a spontaneous vibration overpowering you
Do you dance ecstatic in trance in oblivion,
Balancing the female and male in you?
Let the couple-Yin and Yang
The symbol of the sacred
Cauldron and the Pole—
—female and male energy
Dance in harmony aligning in embrace

Synergising the entirety of the human energy
Sharing in equity the joy of true living!
Ensues in the circle of life perfect fusion
When Yin and Yang harmonise in equal space
Discovering the energy Yang needs in Yin
Yin gains the energy she craves in Yang
Synchronising the heartbeats in unison
Of the lovers in the dance of life!"

4

"I've heard you, my Guru;
The song of Mahamudra
Is beyond all words and symbols
But, I know not yet
How to remain loose and natural
Neither do I want to break the yoke now!

True, might not be, a doer I am
Might be, only a witness I am
I hear a murmur from within often
Not ready for the song of the soul now!
Looking in the mirror of my mind
My alter ego shows up in the reflection
I see our seed budding in her
Winking at me, biting a naughty smile,
Locking it in her sensuous lips!

Not a visitation of spirit
Nor haunting of a ghost
Nor a cursed soul, looking for a body cage
Know not but I've to find out
A name for our unborn seed!

Oh, Guru, I want you only to be my Tilopa
My ideal Guru
Though I'm not accomplished
To be your Naropa
The Ideal disciple, so earnest and loyal!
Let me ask you, my Guru;
Why do I cut the root of the tree now?
And kill the tree forever?
Why do I cut the root of my mind,
And liberate me before tasting the nectar of life?
Might be, you're right,
Life is like licking honey
On the edge of the double-bladed knife
But what can I do when my heart longs for more
And more of the nectar in the flower of life?
Guru, I've to get prepared for the song of the soul
Reciting, learning, de-learning, re-learning
Absorbing the quintessence of experiencing life!

Dreams of Dakinis and Yoginis
Stage dancing in my mind-cosmos

Let me sky-dance with a Red Dakini
The crimson rose sky-dancer
Naked, but covered in jewellery
Wearing a garland of human skulls
Let me loose myself in a tantric dance
To be a perfect conductor, losing all resistance
For the life liquid to flow through my veins!

I like to stare at the dark face of the void---
---Enjoying the beauty of the Black Dakini---
The crow-headed goddess, encompassing
The infinite, silent, black ocean of emptiness!

I'll meditate with Golden Dakini
Sitting on a golden lotus
In the rays of setting, crimson sun
Afloat on deep, blue, green waters
Showering like a golden waterfall
Cascading in breeze of blessings
In the parched gorges of thirst!

I'll dance a ballet
With the green star of power—
—Emerald Dakini
I'll sing karaoke songs, dating Vajrayoginis
Learning and sharing the essence of being!

5

The black sky is cast with clouds--
Thunderbolt, lighting flashing through
Waves of darkness dance with light
In the mysterious ocean!
Deep desires echo in the vale
Passion wakes up, goes for Salsa dancing
Sucking the vital energy from the roots
Tapping on, fine tuning the biorhythms
Lining up the prime energy centres!

A beautiful thought sky-dances
In the milky way of the mind
Enjoying a silent, luminescent
Diamond smile—
Brilliant like the Aurora Borealis!
A long tunnel leads me
To the brilliance of thousand suns
It's time to move fast
In the speed of the mind-waves
Scurrying through the tunnel where
'Bhairavas', the guards who guard the 'Mandala'
Dancing on the earth, wind, fire, and waves!
Deities live at the central temple
At the centre of the 'Mandala'
The sacred geometry

Of the mind and universe—
The sanctified place is drawn to meditate,
Internalising, the purpose of one's being!

Entering through the circle of fire
That consumes ego, envy, desire
Squares of brilliance, guarded doors
Open up the four doors of the 'Mandala'
Snowflakes are reflecting multiple rainbows
Blue, white, red radiance
Stage ballet with rainbows
Reflecting, refracting radiances all the way
Intermingling and intercepting
In the Iceland of the mind-galaxy!

Silence of a diamond smile
Blooms like the rising sun
Surrounded by a red garland
A white damsel is meditating
In lotus posture
A seductive enchantress is she
Watering down the blistering lust
Oh, she's the Vajra Dakini
Nude Diamond White Dakini she is!

In the flowering inferno
Amidst the emerald green leaves

A lotus unfolds its pink petals
A damsel comes out of the life waters
A damsel draped in white translucent robes
Bejewelled body glitters inside the robes
The mystery of the creation is kept secret
Safe at the centre, inside the red flower of life
The most precious jewel of the sacred feminine
Pregnant with the red ruby in her secret cleavage
Looking inside the depth of the labyrinthine path
Towards the dark abyss of the mystery of creation
Meditation only pleases 'Vajrabodhi Dakini'
The seductive enchantress in the silky pure white robes
Reveals secretly the sacred path
To salvation to her ardent devotees!

Ornamented in gold and diamond
The pollen of the flower glitters like pure gold
Immersed in nectar at the centre of the lotus
Mantra is offered to Lord Avalokiteshvara;
Om Ma Ni Pad Me Hum!
Offered mantra of Chenrezig;
Om Mani Peme Hung!
Visualising a Buddha,
And lost in the thought, chanting;
Om Mani Pad Me Hum!
Behold! The Jewel in the Lotus!

I've to imbibe nectar—VAJRAMRITA
Before being blessed by the breeze
Of the brilliant diamond light
And the indestructible
Blue and lilac radiance of Adi-Buddha
I chanted the mantra;
Om Vajrayogini hum phat swaha!
Om Vajrayogini hum phat swaha!
I salute Vajra Dakini—the queen of all the Dakinis
The mystique beauty, offering the key
Of the mysteries of life
The seductive charm that haunts me
Initiates me into the path of self-discovery!
'You're welcome!' said she smiling;
'Spark is to return to the fire, in the end
I'm the emptiness of the diamond mind
Mirroring the infinite cosmos, in your mind
The shining brilliance of pure awareness
That diamond Vajrayogini is me, dancing in you
Pure intellect, shining like thousand suns, leading you
Now you can take your *Vajrayogini* for consummation!'

A few Reflections:

"A religion, even if it calls itself a religion of love, must be hard and unloving to those who do not belong to it."

Sigmund Freud

"What is Tao?
It is just this.
It cannot be rendered into speech.
If you insist on an expression,
This means exactly this."
> **What is Tao?: Lu Tung Pin**

"People are often unreasonable and self-centred. Forgive them anyway.
If you are kind, people may accuse you of ulterior motives. Be kind any way.
If you are honest, people may cheat you. Be honest anyway.
If you find happiness, people may be jealous. Be happy anyway.
The good you do today may be forgotten tomorrow. Do good anyway
Give the world the best you have and it may never be enough. Give your best anyway.
For you see, in the end, it is between you and God. It was never between you and them anyway."
> **Mother Teresa**

"We believe that every being is divine, is God. Every soul is a sun covered over the clouds of ignorance; the difference between soul and soul is owing to the difference in density of these layers of clouds."
> **Swami Vivekananda**

"I like your Christ, I do not like your Christians. Your Christians are so unlike your Christ."
> **Mahatma Gandhi**

"The mandala is an archetypal image whose occurrence is attested throughout the ages. It signifies the wholeness of the Self. This circular image represents the wholeness of the psychic ground or, to put it in mythic terms, the divinity incarnate in man."

Memories, Dreams and Reflections: *Carl Jung*

"Everybody is born in freedom, but dies in bondage. The beginning of life is totally loose and natural, but then enters the society , then enter rules and regulations, morality, discipline and many sorts of trainings, and the looseness and naturalness and the spontaneous being is lost."

Osho

"America and Islam are not exclusive and need not be in competition. Instead, they overlap, and share common principles of justice, tolerance and the dignity of all human beings."

Barrack Obama

"I believe in the religion of Islam. I believe in Allah and peace."

Muhammad Ali

"Whoever goes rightly, does so for his own soul; and whoever goes astray, does so to his own detriment.

Qur'an 17:15

29

Encounter

When he came to her home first time
He knew, she was scared of him
But he said nothing
Just sat on the dining table
Had dinner and gone!

She realized,
Depressing was to live alone
Bored to tears, not a friend to share life
So, she loved DAY
Married WORK
Enjoying loving WORK
More and more
When worn-out
She abandoned DAY at the office
When went home
NIGHT was waiting for her
And followed her
So loyal like her shadow!

Unbolting the front door of her home
She wondered
Who kept the fridge door open?
Who splintered a wine bottle on the floor?
A cracked egg
Separated, from the shell
The golden dome
Sitting over the white fluid pond!

When she opened the locked door
NIGHT felt bashful
Stepping in the bedroom with her
Darkness scampered away, in dread fear
Seeing LIGHT, spewing out of the fluorescent bulbs!

The spur-of-the-moment led her to the bedroom
She was shocked in terror
Followed by NIGHT in horror
He was on her bed with his consort
Enjoying a big mango feast in glee!

Intimidated her by him bullying
Nervous NIGHT could only stare at her in fear
Didn't he take over her house?
After ransacking everything she had?
Shocking her out of her shell?

A few Reflections:

"The serpent is the earthly essence of man of which he is not conscious...It is the mystery that flows to him from the nourishing earth-mother.
The way of life writhes like the serpent from right to left and from left to right, from thinking to pleasure and from pleasure to thinking. Thus the serpent is an adversary and a symbol of enmity, but also wise bridge that connects right and lift through longing, much needed by our life.
                    Red Book: *Carl Jung*

"The shadows have their season, too.
The feathery web the budding maples
cast down upon the sullen lawn
bears but a faint relation to
high summer's umbrageous weight
and tunnel-like continuum
black leached from green, deep pools
wherein a globe of gnats revolves
as airy as an astolabe."
                    Penumbrae: *John Updike*

"The lonesome snag of barbed wire you have wrapped around your heart is cash money, honey, you will have to pay."
                    Ontological: *Maggie Anderson*

30

Is It Time Now?

Ate, not:
Not able to eat:
Taste buds are being eaten away:
Being eaten away;
Even throat, small and large bowels...

Eaten away pancreas:
Bunged up producing insulin;
Thyroids stopped up working,
Fatty liver gets flabby and tubby;
Chubby liver—dead meat—being devoured:
Cirrhosis stops not—eating virgin cells;
Kidneys too surrender gradually.

Breathe not:
Lungs are being eaten away;
Withering away lungs,
Unable to hold breath of life...
Pump not blood:
Bleeding heart is being eaten away....

Unable to pump blood of life,
Arteries, veins, nerves dig up dead beat
But continued continuous eating
Hungry cancer cells:
Continued, eating her hungry belly;
Consuming her completely:
He mumbled; "Fight it out my love;
Don't go away,
Stem cells and cloning are there
To save you
Nano-robots are on job
To exterminate
Those monstrous germs!

The ventilators will keep you for a while
Dear, you'll be fine
Even out of the ICU
It is time for you
To find the God-particle in you:
I love you, Now!
More than I ever loved you so far!

Let me hold your hand
Keep close to my heart
Tear drops roll down
Choked heart continued mumbling
"Cheer up: you're going to be fine:

It's not yet time to fly away,
Leaving me, my chirpy bird of love –
You're going to be treated well
Body tissues are reviving
Cloning guys are working hard here
To repair those lost organs
The best of the best master robots
And Robot-Doctors are serving you
Experienced in bringing life out of dead cells!
Medical history will be re-written
WE WILL WIN—WWW
This war of good over the evil
A world without war and disease
For healthy, peaceful, joyful living!

A few Reflections:

*"Remember me when I am gone away,
Gone far away into the distant land;
When you can no more hold me by the hand,
Nor I half turn to go, yet turning stay."*
　　　　　　　Remember: *Christina Rossetti*

"Hope is the thing with feathers
That perches in the soul,
And sings the tune without the words,
And never stops at all."

Emily Dickinson

"It was passed from one bird to another,
the whole gift of the day.
The day went from flute to flute,
went dressed in vegetation,
in flights which opened a tunnel
through the wind would pass
to where birds were breaking open
the dense blue air –
and there, night came in."

Bird: *Pablo Neruda*

" Once you choose hope, anything's possible."

Christopher Reeve

"When you come to the end of your rope, tie a knot and hang on"

Franklin D. Roosevelt

"Because we are interested in promoting wellness, we will integrate medicine with performing arts, arts and crafts, agriculture, recreation, nature, and social service."

Patch Adams

31

My Name is c-Myc

The Reflection
In the bathroom mirror
Stares at you,
Saying that the feminine figurine,
Chiselled in marble
Is not Venus; but you:
Mammography has eyes,
To see lumps, beneath the skin,
Growing dangerously, somewhere,
In the dark crevices of the tissues!

You feel
Shadows crawl
Beneath your fair skin
Like a crab stinging and oozing through
Consuming the delicate tissues
On the walls of your womb
Spreading, growing and expanding
Giving unbearably, painful lesions
Octopus' tentacles feed on all over the body!

In the dark corners are the spiders
Weaving relentlessly webs all over
Showing off, bloody vampire fangs
Through microscope magnifying those
Razor-sharp claws, piercing nails,
Biting, and tearing off
Delicate body tissues
Wolfing down, you....
Your physique, psyche, spirits at one go!

Let the Robot-Doctor look for it
The panacea hides somewhere
Like a shadow, behind the veil
We've to look for the cure
Kept in the unknown freezer chambers
Of the new medicines
Till research is fully ready
And the eggs in you—
Those human oocycles
—are kept safely in crypto-preservation!

2

Let me confess before you
I'm a gene –
My name is c-MYC –
I control cell division

Mutate and grow, causing death
To the human body!
I keep one signal----
To turn on cell growth, uncontrolled
I've another signal to operate,
For ordering cell's destruction!

You must know
Cells are programmed to die
To keep you alive!
1,000 million cells die,
In an hour in your body,
To keep you alive till it's time,
Balancing between cell division,
And cell death in your body!
But, some cells forget
How to die,
Eat to live immortal
Divide, multiply in procreation,
Growing exponentially,
In dangerous proportion;
Finally killing you in cold blood
And that's the problem!

I'm a Robot-Doctor-Cop,
Doing my job to save you
I'm going to teach

The tumour-cells--c-MYC
Growing in you
The most important lesson
They forgot—how to die
And there lies the secret of your cure!

But, remember, I should know
How to teach the cancer cells that lesson
And make them follow the lesson
And that's our problem, the humanity's problem
Medical research's challenge!
You might die or not
To come back alive from a coma or not
Depend solely on that key to unlock the mystery
The scientists' ability to decode the obscurity
And discover the cure
Opening the nature's chamber of secrets!

A few Reflections:

"Can it be you that I hear? Let me view you, then,
Standing as when I drew near to the town
Where you would wait for me, yes, as I knew you then,
Even to the original air-blue gown!"
                              The Voice: *Thomas Hardy*

"It is not the years in your life that counts but the life in your years."
Abraham Lincoln

"Time is shortening. But every day that I challenge this cancer and survive is a victory for me."
Ingrid Bergman

"I think it's important for me as an actor that I say these are the issues I'm going to be committed to. One of them for me is women and children's health around the world and their rights; the other is ovarian cancer."
Nicole Kidman

"Stem cell therapies have the potential to do for chronic diseases what antibiotics did for infectious diseases. It is going to take years of serious research to get there, but as a neurologist, I believe the prospect for a 'penicillin' for Parkinson's is a potential breakthrough that we must pursue. As in other areas of creative endeavour in science, the answers will come only with careful experimentation."
Dean of the Faculty of Medicine at Harvard University: Joseph Martin

"As people of faith we are called to be partners with God in healing and in the alleviation of human pain and suffering. With careful regulation, we affirm the use of stem cell tissue for research that may result in the restoring of health to those suffering from serious illness."
Presbyterian Church, United States

32

Blood Swimming Marines

Mom,
Your greenish eyes are beautiful
Though, lost their glow
Due to illness
Let me send in you
A few battalions
Of the blood swimming marines
To save you!

Let them swim
Through the arteries and veins
And dive deep and swim
Into the blood streams in the aorta
To enter into your heart!

Let them pass through
The capillary streams
Into your lungs
Seeing through their camera eyes
Carrying medicines, tools and armaments!

They'll reach
Every cell of your body
Wagging their swimming tail fins
Their sensors are sharp and focussed
Nothing can escape
From their intense scrutiny!

Believe me,
They're the NANO robotic marines
Trained in reaching all hideouts
Of the enemies, even in sanctuaries
Even in the bone marrow!

They'll fight to the last
And we will win the war
Against those deadly disease germs
Defeat them, exterminate them,
Repair and re-build
Those damaged cells and tissues;
Defending all the gates
Of the City of Nine Gates
And re-build a new beautiful you
From the stem cells, my dear mom!

A few Reflections:

"There is another sky,
Ever serene and fair
And there is another sunshine,"
                  There is another sky: *Emily Dickinson*

"Hope – Hope in the face of difficulty. Hope in the face of uncertainty. The audacity of hope!"
                                  Barrack Obama

33

Visible God

In the morning,
The Visible God salutes the Sun
While clambering up the hilltop
Scaling the eastern horizon
Overlooking the valley
And romancing with Day!

Golden rays fill in his eyes
Lungs are full, inhaling cool breeze
Mind is filled with hope to the brim
Heart, spills over love
Body is fully charged in energy!

The workshop gets busy, as usual,
In repairing and overhauling
The engines of life that slow down,
Indisposed to pump,
Blood-oil to flow, not so smooth,
To keep the vehicle of life moving,
Along the indefinite terrains!

The public speculate;
'Isn't he a robot of a doctor?
Or a young doctor of a robot?
Or an engineer-cum-magician?
Giving life to the engines of life?
We'll call him our Visible God on earth!

There's magic in his hands
To do God's job at ease
Fixing feeble hearts---
De-clogging, de-plaqueing,
Doing angioplasty, angiography,
To many a fragile, ragged,
Congested, tapered hearts!

Little did he care
The throbbing pain, growing in his heart,
While he's busy fixing others' hearts!
Why should shadows chase?
When light is in romance?

Nobody knows,
When the last tick of life ticks,
May be the moment,
When the previous tick ends,
That spark, ignited life in you,
In your mom's womb:

When X Y chromosomes,
Had their honeymoon!
Everything ends,
At the zero point,
Merging into nothingness,
The being becoming a non-being!

The full Moon sleeps cool,
Fatigued after night long
Lovemaking with night,
Leaves in hurry,
The valley of the sky,
Only in the day break!

The full moon unfurls a silvery carpet
Swanky over boisterous sea waves
Bridging a shimmering waterway to the Moon
To welcome the Visible God to the divine abode
Heart—stop not pumping!
Lungs—stop not breathing!
Pulse—stop not beating!
Brain—stop not in command!
Don't let our Visible God go!

The full moon moves forward,
To kiss the urging waves of desire,
Waves leap forward
For hugging the moon

Coming out of the dreadful
Depth of the Ocean;
'It's not time for you
To come to the Vale of Bliss
You're the Visible God
For many a star-crossed soul!
Go for a deeper breath, you doc,
But not the final one,
But the one you begin,
To take care of your heart too
To be able to take care of others!

Your heart is pumping back to life
Your godly grin of love is back in place
You're distributing perfume of kindness
All around you, in abundance,
Your patients are around you, doc;
Praying for your heart to pump life in you
We all adore you, our Visible God!

A few Reflections:

"It isn't until you come to a spiritual understanding of who you are – not necessarily a religious feeling, but deep down, the sprit within – that you can begin to take control."

Oprah Winfrey

*"Yes, yes,
that's what
I wanted,
I always wanted.
I always wanted,
to return
to the body
where I was born."*

Song: *Allen Ginsberg*

"A society is judged by the way it cures for its most vulnerable citizens. As an American, I am ashamed that we have turned out backs on millions of our children. I want to do my part to rectify this terrible situation."

Marlo Thomas

"The thought that life could be better is woven indelibly into our hearts and our brains."

Paul Simon

34

Kiss of Fire

When a candle is kissed,
By fire:
The candle becomes fire!
Fire then blossoms into a flower
The fiery flower
Takes over
The candle forever!

Before that flower is faded,
The fire is extinguished,
Prior to the end of the candle,
Let the flames heat,
The frozen hearts!
And let the light,
Enlighten the clammy spirits,
Driving away those devils,
Hiding in the dark cranny of the mind!

Let the power in the fire
Let loose,

Into the locked horizon of the self,
Engulfing the phoney smugness, extending,
A new-fangled cologne in the air!

When fire devours fiercely,
Everything in terrible appetite,
Fire gulps down even the funeral pyre,
Consuming disease germs,
Viruses, bacteria, fungi,
And cancer cells, as well!
If still, left free, not putting off,
Fire eats away thoughts that infect
The good intellect, making it dead
Till the end, sooner than the soul flies
To light a new candle of life
Purifying body, mind, thought and spirit in fire!

A few Reflections:

"The gold moth did not love him
So gorgeous, she flew away.
But the gray moth circled the flame
Until the break of day
And then, with wings like a dead desire,
She fell, fire-caught, into the flame."
      Fire-Caught: *Langston Hughes*

35

Awakening the Serpent

Silence speaks, it's got tongue
Listen to the silence and
The music of silence
Before the thundery typhoon
Absorbs the intense energy flow –
The soft chiming of the soul!
Fine tune, to listen to the reverberations
From the consecrated shrine!

Isn't it time for you to invoke 'KUNDALINI',
The somnolent spine-snake power,
Curling, and clinging at the base of the spine?
You'll discover the life energy
Dissolved in you, the cosmic energy that flow:
You may name her Goddess SHAKTI,
She's quiescent in deep slumber
Like a foetus in the mother's womb!

Go slow, lest she gets perturbed;
But surely do wake her up, inducing,

Energise—Cheer her up; and let her awaken you;
Searching for her consort, traversing upwards,
Along your spine, over the energy circles,
Joining them, aligning and de-blocking,
In search of her consort, SHIVA;
Living at the top of the mount
That's the crown chakra on your head!

Come; let us sit in the yogic posture
In harmony with our being, light a smile
Aligning the seven energy circles
Keep breathing good thoughts in fresh air
Getting ready witnessing Kundalini arising
Traversing along the vital life forces!

Let us chant the root mantras
Let mantras resonate in the air
Consoling our mind, cooling our heart
And chilling the soul to be calm
Listen to the vibrations in the thin air
Continue chanting the Shakti seed mantras
Let us build the supreme energy flow in us!

YAM for Anahata Chakra
RAM for Manipura Chakra
LAM, SHAM, VAN for Muladhara Chakra
AIM, HREEM, KLEEM, SHREEM

Let Shakti—the vital energy begin to move
And help her reach the crown chakra
Let her merge in perfect union with Shiva
May thousand lotuses bloom in their union!
Blessed be you; enlightened like a Buddha
Synchronising the energy circles to the intellect!

A few Reflections:

"Reality can be experienced only with the eye of understanding, not just by a scholar. What the moon is like must be seen with one's own eyes. How can others do it for you?
Adi Shankaracharya

"God is in all men, but all men are not in God; that is why we suffer."
Swami Ramakrishna Paramahamsa

"In prayer it is better to have a heart without words than words without a heart"
Mahatma Gandhi

"Every bud has all that it needs to be a flower."
Sri Sri Ravishankar

"We alone stay
While years hurry on,
The flower fared forth, though its fragrance still stays."
Petals: *Amy Lowell*

36

Champagne Party in the Milky Way

"Hello, my name is Stephen Hawking, physicist, cosmologist and something of a dreamer. Although I cannot move and I have to speak through a computer, in my mind I am free."
"I do believe in time travel - Time travel to the future. Time flows like a river and it seems each of us is carried relentlessly along the time's current."

Professor Stephen Hawking

1

"Dear Marilyn, you may see me
Physically confronted, senses bundled up,
Immobile I may be on this special chair;
But in mind, I've got senses; ears, eyes, and nose,
Tongue, sensitive skin and sharp sixth sense too!
Bear in mind,
In the womb of misfortune,
Always waits---a golden egg to be fertilized;
To give birth hope for the future!
Come Marilyn, let us go partying now
You're invited to my champagne party

I'll ride you in my time machine,
Zooming through the time tunnel
Into time, into space
Into the fourth dimension
Cruising along the River of Time...

Why don't you note the venue of the party?
At the Cosmic Strip,
Near the other end of the Cosmos,
(Up to you, if you think there's an end),
Of the Spiralling Galaxy:
At Café Eye of Horus,
Old Time Canyon on the Galaxy Highway
Opposite to the Star Space Yacht Club
Next to Granny Black Hole!
Don't miss the exact
Time-Space-Coordinates";
Invited Mr. Stephen Hawking,
Famous living cosmologist,
To the legendary Hollywood actress,
Of yester era flame—Ms. Marilyn Monroe!

"Oh, Stevie, I love to be in your party
You---naughty, brilliant, dreamer,
You prefer blondes, yeah? Some like it too hot!
You're the most imaginative fantasist,
Hold me tight Sweetie; I'll sit on your lap,

Don't you mind, Isn't it a little scary?
But you can drive me crazy,
Aboard your cute piece of equipment!

Tell me, Stevie; what's that restaurant, you said?
Eye of Horus
Can I eat Horus Eyes fried in chilli sauce
At that Egyptian joint with red wine?
You've to spend for me my Cute-Pie,
For chatting with the best of the best sex siren
Ever born in the universe!

May be after, I'll take a little time out
To visit my grandma,
Wouldn't you mind, driving me there too?
My brainy baby, I'll love you solo
A hot kiss for you solo
That you've not tasted ever in your life!"
Flirted Marilyn!

"Don't you like a rollercoaster ride?
I'll drive you in an ultra-modern Wormhole
Speeding along the length of the Time-Canyon
To the other end of the universe
Only one promise, babe; lose not your temper,
Shoot not your granny out of any irritation
Trust me; I go for time travel quite often,

You know, I've dated Cleopatra on the sly,
Ha, ha, duping barmy Caesar and nutty Antony!"

"You're wayward, wilful kernel,
Do you conjure I buy your story?"

"Believe me, baby; time travel isn't a heresy
I'm a physicist, not an eccentric,
Nor a fantastic, fanatic, hoodwink either;
You can enjoy time travelling with me,
To the dark cavern of the cosmic origin
Into the past or into the infinite future
Enjoying never-ending honeymoon
In the present in our wormhole!"
Reassured Stephen; winking,
With a twinkle in his green eyes"!

"Steve, take me with you,
Train me; please; let's make love
While swimming in this River of Time
Against the flow,
Towards the origin of the Time River
Near the mouth of the Lake Abyss –
That Black Lake of Oblivion
Let us visit our great, great grandma
Living on the banks of the Lake Abyss
Our common African Black Granny!"

"I'll take you everywhere
Grandpa Adam and Grandma Eve too
Don't feel shy if you find them, fully naked,
Shamelessly, indulging in love-lust games!"

"But, I'll not forbid them that,
But forbid eating that goddamn fruit
I should chase Satan out of the Garden of Eve
I'll use your gun, if need be,
It's sure, I won't allow him
Playing his cheating games,
Manoeuvring innocent Eve granny by trickery"!

"Marilyn, don't be tempted
To dress up the naked truth
Why cover up
The face of history behind a veil?
Why do you want to change
The course of history?
Don't you ever dare take out
Your sniper gun to shoot our nanny?
And cause to change
The course of the River of Time!"

"Stevie, why am I finding
My soul so hungry?
Urging to merge

The Ocean of Love?
I'll join Krishna
On his bed of Milk-Ocean
Beneath the umbrella-hood
Of the Infinity-Serpent
Pressing the points on his feet
Doing reflexology and acupuncture
Learning the magic cure
From the Yellow Emperor
Enjoying immortality of love with the lord!

He's cool, bright and breezy
Both in war and love, alike;
In high spirits, frolicking with women;
Living always in their heart,
Helping them in need,
Like soul and supreme consciousness,
In the ultimate dance of bliss,
Liquefying soul in the symphony!"

"We must attend Jesus' Sermon on the Mount
After attending to Buddha's
First sermon after enlightenment!"

"Stevie, I do want my Jesus smiling,
Not so melancholic, not to be crucified
He had taken too much pain for the sinners

I want him to enjoy life, and of course,
Save him from those criminals!
I wish to sit beside him on the banks
Of the River of the Past, overflowing
From the Lake - Black Oblivion!

I like sleeping with Napoleon
He'll be fantastic—a war horse in action
I would bear him a baby Bonaparte
To set this fanatical world of terrorism upright
Mothering a philosopher king
To rule this world
Justly, as nobody ever did
I'll love him more than Josephine,
I want him, not to be defeated and gone
From the scene after the Battle of Waterloo!"

"Marilyn, do you think
You can save John F Kennedy?
Never to get him assassinated
By an unknown bullet!
Do you mind begetting
A few kids from him too?
Marilyn, do I've to vouchsafe,
You're awfully sexy in the cosmos,
But I'm afraid, isn't your brain
A little shallow –

A little bent hollow sphere?
Do you think anyone will ever
Be authorized, to tinker history?
You might enjoy that risky reverie
Shooting your grandma and what not
That matters, baby a lot,
Wouldn't have deprived the world of you
I've some doubts, some equations
Are itching on my head, but I've to ask Einstein,
Hasn't he made some miscalculations?
I've to find out answer to the problem!"

"Oh, Stevie, I know, you're great
But I've got an idea,
Why shouldn't we chat?
With the famous 'Naked Fakir?'
He would be smiling all the way
A giant saint experimenting with life!
I want to learn from him;
How to diffuse the nuclear weapons
Doing non-stop, non-violence!
He'll be my chosen Guru
For making Non-Cooperation arsenal
To fight against injustice?
Isn't he cute in his toothless smile?
Hey Ram; I would be sad,

If I'm not able to save him
From the bullet of his children!

Haven't you invited, Stevie?
My hero artist—Michaelangelo
What a sculpture is his David!
What a perfect male nude idol!
Just like my cute Miki, I suppose.
I've irrepressible crush on Mike's muscles
I'll kiss him in front of everyone
You silly scientist; don't be envious, cutie;
Instead you should ask him
Had he sculpted himself as David?"

"Don't forget to ask about the Holy Grail
When we meet Leonardo
I get goose pimples over my soul
Dreaming the script in the eyes of Mona Lisa
What a heart winning smile is it!
A perfect painting of bliss
I'll find out from Jesus
About his beloved disciple John!"

"But, Stevie, I've to ask you one thing,
Aren't you paranoid with time travel?
Aren't you a schizophrenic?
You mumble often,

You see wormholes,
In every nook and cranny!
Aren't you getting some syndrome?
Marilyn's giggle resonated
In the hollow underbelly of the Milky Way!

"Don't make fun of me, Big Baby;
It's not obsession, it isn't funny either,
I see wormholes everywhere,
You've to trust a scientist
Who proves what he says,
I believe in creating a portal to the past,
A portal to the future,
And a portal to the present!
Didn't I do that?

Come, Marilyn,
We've no time to waste for any gibberish
Climb on into the cockpit of my Wormhole,
Along with me, babe,
Carefully bringing your soft body aboard;
Let us fly, fly far, far, far away;
You and me together flying
Till the end of the universe!

I've been waiting for so long
For this lovely moment to come

Let us fly into the infinite spiralling galaxies
Cruising through the time canyon
Toward the Cosmic Strip discotheque!"

2

"I love picnicking
With high-density-brainy guys,
I'm fully ready; show me, now,
The path to the fourth dimension of time!
Stevie, where's your space vehicle?
Where's your giant Wormhole?
Or whatever Goddamn hole,
You're obsessed with?"

"Look at my left, look at my right,
Look at my front, look at my back,
Look above, look below, look everywhere;
Wormholes are flying, crisscrossing the galaxies
Let me put you now in the fourth dimension!
Once we fly away, as you desire,
Dreaming on bed with me,
Who knows? When will we emerge?
And where?"

"But, tell me, Steve,
Where's your space vehicle?

How can we fly into time?
Without a time engine?
How'll you thank Galileo?
For telescoping the heavens?
How'll we find out?
The end of our love story?
Where will it be hiding
In the time-grotto?"

"Marilyn, see those tiny wrinkles
Crevices and voids in time
Smaller than molecules
Smaller than even atoms
Those sub-atomic particles
See quarks, leptons, protons...
Right now, I see the quantum foam!

Let me capture now
A wormhole for you
But, I've to enlarge it, baby,
To make it big enough for us
To time-rafting through the time river
Navigating the wormhole yacht
Zooming through the other end of the cosmos!"

"You're too astounding, EVE-Inspiring
Show me, that worm vehicle thing,

I suppose I should love that
That hole you've been talking all along
To detour around the galaxies!
I admire you Steve, a lot,
But I'm infatuated to another Steve too
What perfect jobs he did for all of us!
What an enticing Apple did he make!
That iPod, iPhone, iPad maker I adore
Am I not seeing him with a new job now
Riding on the bundle of white clouds?
Cloud computing for GPS?
The Galaxy Positioning System
For navigating the galaxies?"

"Come on, Marilyn
Don't talk of anyone now
I'm the one and only one
Prof. Stephen Hawking
You should know and you must care
I could be hypersensitive at times
A crack, horribly jealous many a time
When you do rubbing on my Sixth sense
Making me grow green-horns with envy!
Let me date you exclusively
This is my day,
I carved out this evening with you
It is me who've got you here

In the spiralling galaxies
I'll hold you tight,
While showing you nebulae,
Energy sucking big black holes,
You bet, it's the best date
You can ever imagine
No boyfriend of you could ever take you
A ride like this by a wormhole
It needs celebration
Let me give you a kiss of your lifetime!"

"Stephen, you're too eccentric
But I don't see anything
Except drifting white cotton clouds
Am I getting blind, you mean?
Where's your mysterious wormhole?"

"Yes, now I can visualise,
I own this wormhole solo
Look at the smallest, cutest thing
It can become a giant wormhole
Flying into the hollow womb
Of the Mother Universe
Moving along the tunnel
Towards the unknown future
It should take us
To the farthest end of the time canyon!

Marilyn Baby, aren't you seeing
Those ferocious cannibals?
Oh, Jesus Christ!
Aren't they Anti-Dinosaurs?
More brutal than Dinosaurs?
Charging against our wormhole?
Oh, Marilyn, come close;
Hug me firmly, I'm soul-scared,
I love that way babe, when I'm afraid!

Oh, Jesus, I forget I'm an atheist so often,
Oh Science! The power of knowledge!
Save us from these unruly beasts of humanity!
What's happening to our time contraption?
Isn't it somersaulting into the scary gorges?

Let me enlarge the wormhole,
I've to pilot this space-shuttle
To anchor near the Galaxy Rivera
Let us escape hoodwinking,
Those energy-sucking black holes!
Let me now ride the wormhole
Fast...Faster and faster...
Help me in navigating it speedier,
Just keep titillating me, nicely
So that I can accelerate the machine
To two thousand times of Apollo 10

The fastest of the manned vehicles
So far in the cosmos
Don't be shy hugging me,
Marilyn, I just love soft touch!"

"I'm with you my Stevie,
You've got licence to flirt with me,
But, show me everything
If you want to have fun with me!
You can take me to your bedroom
Bath me in the best of the perfumes
I'll be in your wormhole cockpit
Afloat over the Cosmic Ocean Spa!
But you go fast, faster than any man
Ever could do it with me
Fly in the speed of my mind waves,
Faster and still faster...
Blessed be you, the fastest you be
Fly me; you to the very end
Of the infinite spiralling galaxies!"

3

"Let me pour some champagne for you
Let me open the door, thereafter!
Miss Universe of the Future
Is knocking at my door

I'd invited her too for this party
I've to finish, some more experiments!"

"Stephen, are you awake?
I don't understand you
Are you conscious?
Are you dreaming?
I can't believe you any more
Nobody has turned up
For your champagne party
From the heavens above
What a shame on Earth!"

"Marilyn, but you should know
These wormholes are pretty tricky
Even to see them in our mind
We're still possibly living only
In the three-dimensional world
Probably you're in the fourth dimension
But I wish to take you
To the eleventh dimension of the M-theory"

"Oops! Steve, you're beyond me
You have too much IQ and EQ
But I have only BQ—the Beauty Quotient";
Acknowledged Marilyn Monroe

"Believe me; it is all because.....
Because......."
"Steve; what do you mean?
Because of me...?
I would have dated other Steve";
Screamed, Marilyn!

"Forget that Steve, I say
You're damned with me now
Enjoy the ride in my Wormhole
You should learn something new
Like the grandfather paradox,
The Mad Scientist paradox,
Why did they stop us from time travel?
But, if you don't tell anyone
I'll whisper in your ears,
The secret key to time travel!"

"That's cool, tell me, Stevie,
I'm good at keeping secrets
You've the most beautiful mind;
And you trust me a lot!
I'll listen to you, like a good friend,
Even if I understand nothing!
You sound, starry-eyed;
I love your brilliant diamond mind
Now I can see those luminous nebulae

Winking at me in the Milky Way";
Marilyn kissed Steve in his mouth.

"Marilyn, now, you see that guy
He's a mad scientist, watch him
He's standing in a time tunnel:
Just stretching one minute into the past
Hoorah! The mad scientist sees himself...
Oh, Jesus, why do you come
To rescue even the non-believers?
Look at that mad scientist
He is facing him one minute before?
Alas! I can't believe, Marilyn!
He shot him... the earlier himself...
In the flow of the cosmic River of Time
Yes, using that goddamn wormhole
He's dead and gone with his wormhole
Swallowed by the black hole of time!"

"Hey Mr. Stephen, I'm scared
Why should he shoot his earlier himself?
You're quite a bit psychic,
I don't trust you anymore
What sort of time tour of the cosmos is this?
Now, you tell me,
Why did he shoot him and when?"
Enquired, Marilyn!

"It's the problem –
The nightmare of the time traveller
I need a chalk and black board
To write the right Mathematical equations
But I cannot move now!
You must listen to me keenly,
It could be the wormhole
Do you believe me, Marilyn?
The story of time travel isn't yet over?"

4

"Huh! Oh, Yeah! Please,
Is there something still?
But pour for me, more of champagne
Your story will become exciting,
Only if I'm a bit intoxicated,
I'm now fully bowled out of my senses!"
"Enjoy every molecule
Of the best exotic champagne;
And forget not, holding me tight,
Even if you're not scarred,
I'm frightened, without your warmth
I'm like Bacchus, love good drinks,
Too delicious to resist, but;
Pardon me, there's a bit of a hitch,
I can't pour it for you,

My hedonistic, voluptuous girlfriend
Until we're aboard the time machine!"

"Oh! Gosh! I know you're weird
But, I thought,
You're not so absolutely loopy!"

"If you don't understand me
It's a syndrome of your void brain
Listen, satellites orbit the Earth
Time runs faster in those clocks
Not that the clock is inaccurate:
But because time runs faster,
Faster than on the Earth, in the space,
That's why we correct
Clocks in the space shuttles
I've to ask Einstein about drags on time
And show the calculations I made and be sure!"

5

"Steve, I've got a severe migraine now
Only if you pour more champagne
Should my brain be capable to re-focus?
On the exciting journey, we're in, in the hole?"

"Marilyn, when we fly
Right into the centre of the Milky Way
Just about twenty six thousand light years away
There lies, the heaviest object in the galaxy
A super massive black hole:
Mass of four million suns
Crushed down into a single point
Amazing giant of a black hole
So intense is its gravitational pull
Dragging even light into its centre!

Let me confide in you some secret:
For the crew in that spaceship,
Orbiting the black hole,
Time is not able to walk in normal speed,
Slows down, by half, or even lesser
I want you to be with me in that spaceship
Orbiting the black hole with me!
I'll pour for you more champagne
While we launch to the galaxies
We'll have never ending gala-trip
Boogie jumping in the Time-waterfall
River rafting in the waves of Time-River
I'll dance with you, singing Madonna songs
I'm open in this wormhole to justify my love

I never met anyone like this, I'm crazy for you
Don't tell me to stop, and love isn't true
Can you feel the weight of my passion in your heart?
I want to express my love, make you feel
Like a virgin, oh, ooh, ah, ooh for the first time
An empress on the throne, ruling the wormhole
I'll be like a child, whispering softly in your ears
I won't preach, I know, you're a material girl,
I'll get into the groove to prove my love
Baby, open your heart; I want to be there forever
Take me there, like a prayer,
With no end, no beginning!

Sorry I'm, badly immobile; I need your help, babe
I've lost my voice; you've to be my voice, my love
But I promise, when we return to the Planet Earth
We'll see our children and grandchildren
Aged like our great, grandfathers
They might age double, triple, quadruples...
When we would almost stop aging
Pulling the legs of Time,
Making Time limping, ha, ha...
And we'll have lots and lots of fun
Endless honeymoons in the galaxies
Always as fresh and new
Like a virgin ever in space
Let me confide in you,

A secret; Marilyn Comeliness
That super massive black hole
Is a real time machine!"

"Oh, yeah, Steve
I'll sing a Michael Jackson for you
There's a place for you in my heart
You can heal the world, change the world
And make this world a better place for all
We'll fly so high, spirits don't die
We'll see in the mirror of our mind
How we look like, be not hypocritical
Discover the power in us
You're not alone, you don't stop
Till we get there; I promise
You'll get enough of me
We can beat those who spoil our mission
I'll sing a Britney for you now
Losing my control, baring my soul
I'll fight with them like a karate kid
They'll look small up from here
I love you and I care, promise,
Don't leave me ever
To be left to me; myself, and I;
Promise me, you won't be a sinner,
Cheating on me, crazy for your love

We'll dance to the best
Of the music band and tune!

Stevie, can't I joke with you, my man?
There's something that alerts my mind
I can understand now
A bit of the mad scientist paradox;
Because, he must be an oddball like you!
Is your story of the time travel not yet over?";
Beseeched, Marilyn Monroe, in despair!

"Listen to me, babe, please,
I need your awareness, chock-a-block
To bring the power of your brain enough
To grapple the exciting last part
If you're ready to travel with me so high
Really, really, very, very fast
In the womb of the galaxy
Faster than the speed of light
Not being sucked up by any black holes
We'll take only one way ticket to future!
Let us board a superfast time-train,
Let us travel at the speed of light
Nay at the speed of our mind waves
Don't you worry; your Stevie will stick to you
Let the time train encircle the Earth
Over and over, seven times a second

Let time decelerate for us
I don't care, as long as you're with me
Not even a glass of red wine, I need!"

"Stevie, did you propose to marry me?
I forget; has anyone erased my memory?
Have we made it legal, I don't know; possibly,
I'm too much intoxicated by now!"

"You know, Marilyn, believe me,
We've built something of a train,
The world's largest particle accelerator
Yes, at CERN in Geneva in Switzerland,
If you don't believe me, I'll show you
Come with me to Switzerland!"

"Stevie, why are we moving to Switzerland?
What happened to our wormhole honeymoon?
Aren't we in the cockpit of your wormhole?
Tell me, are we not yet in that damn hole?"

"Oh, don't argue, baby, anger plunders beauty
Hurry up; there's no time for balderdash
We've to board the Time Train, mind you.
We won't ride the wormhole anymore
I don't want you to be in any risky hole
To be sucked by any hungry black hole!"

"Oh! Jesus Christ! I had enough of this crank,
Hey, you, great genius of a cosmologist
Pour for your beauty, now I say,
Some real champagne in a real party!"

"That shouldn't be an issue
You're my special guest
Let me propose to you
Will you marry me, Marilyn?
We'll go for partying all over the cosmos
Endlessly in its infinite skies
Encircling the spiralling galaxies!
Marilyn; am I in for some phantasm?
Making extra giant wormhole in delirium?
Flying for honeymooning only you and me?
Going superfast, duping and zeroing down time?
Being extra-smart to be immortal like Gods?
And you must know that giant worm hole
Is going to be really the time machine, I told you
Oh, yah, I'll pour more champagne for you
But, Marilyn, I'm afraid; and terribly sorry too;
Aren't you in the fourth dimension these days?
Do you believe in your Stevie? Isn't it real my baby?
I'm yet in the third dimension; don't you worry;
We'll try travelling on time in a time-engine, together
So high to the eleventh dimension
Of the M-Theory, the mother of all theories
My equations are getting right, you must know!"

A few Reflections:

"A rose-yellow moon in pale sky
When the sunset is faint vermillion
In the mist among the tree-boughs
At thou to me, my beloved."
       Images: *Richard Aldington*

"When I'm out there, in time, I am inverted, changed into a desperate version of myself. I become a thief, a vagrant, an animal who runs and hides. I startle old woman and amaze children. I am a trick, an illusion of the highest order, so incredible that I am actually true."
  The Time Traveller's Wife: *Audrey Niffenegger*

A few Reflections

BOOK 3

Kalki's War Against The Antichrist

37

Holy Unholy Land

1

This is the primordial,
Holy unholy terra firma,
Hackneyed for its misrule,
By a purblind-ancient King and
His old-fashioned,
Husband-worshipping,
Blindfolded Queen,
Who gave birth a lump of flesh,
Cut into hundred pieces,
Kept in a pot, covered,
To make the first hundred
Test-tube pot babies!!

Didn't the couple
Mollycoddle injustice?
And massacre truth,
Causing a war of the titans,
The Good versus the Evil—

—the epic Battle of Mahabharata,
At Kurukshetra—
The temple town in India;
And in the ensuing warfare every moment,
At the temple of our mind!

Fire-spewing tarragons
Infest everywhere, here
But Fire-Eaters and Fire-Fighters are few!
Hoh! There you're! MANGO people—
—Quite humdrum ordinary folks;
Guys know only to vote,
But not even knowing,
How to fast, not to die, but to win!

Nay, it is not yet a 'banana republic'
But, what's there, for anyone to get flabbergasted
If rulers here, go berserk, blind, impoverished of vision
Stone-deaf, tongue-tied, comatose at one go!
Why do we fast, trying to die on the streets?
Why do we put fire on us and our family?
When injustice takes us at ignition point
Don't we know poverty is seldom killed by fire?
Mahatma was shot by us and sent to ether world
And we are his disciples, assumed as phoney dolls
Fluky to escape afterlife in blitzkrieg against justice!

2

In the tainted environs,
The blood-sucking vermin burgeon
Like lethal, killing Dengue, and other parasites
Breed in billions like termites eating the host
Exploring every pockmark and fissure!

Swarms of mosquitoes attack like terrorists
Blood thirsting, knowing only one job,
Ever ready for assault with no provocation
But gunning lust for fresh blood thrills
Hanker after vulnerable, innocent lives
Hanging around over the head humming
A sadistic note before launching
A deadly 360-degree ambush at anytime
In a take the blood or die killing subterfuge!

These guerrilla bombers sense our carbon print
Love to attack the way we live, sensing the human scent
Tracking smell of sweat, odour of breath
Goodnight sleep is good for vampires
Munching us in horde, sucking our blood
Those guerrillas love to kill family and pets too
The Asian Tiger group of militants
Assail not at night but prefer striking at day time
Do you want to donate more blood to the militants?

Those mutant antihuman beasts thrive
Laying their eggs out of our blood
Can we enjoy life, dancing in Gangnam Style
Live rocking and tapping on the floor, singing
Howling Hoh-Hoh-ing and Gaga-Gaga-ing
But wielding counter weapons, shielding us
Lest we fall as victims to the faceless bloodshed
Helplessly hit by swarms of bloody criminals
In the chronic everyday and night nightmare
Fighting poverty, disease and exploitation, terrorism
Those who defile minds, desecrate milieu, kill humanism
Beget an archetypal environ, for malfeasance to boom
All set, to do away with life, in unscrupulous finesse
In an esoteric, erratic, terrifying stillness
Unlike the blood sucking, humming, tiny midgets!

Some might argue, what's the dilemma, anyway
One day, you've to die, wherever you're
How do you die; is it guaranteed anywhere?
Indubitably, stage-settings are fine-tuned here
To hand-carry you, fast dying, in many a moment
Happily escorting you, to the final exit before time
And you'll die pretty younger;
If you're badly off, though not so bland,
As the dog-hungry, Sub-Saharan fraternity!
In this dubious, incredible ancient land

Innumerable Gods and Goddesses
Domicile in temples
We had revolutions—bloodless
Green Revolution, White Revolution
And loads of blood-shedding...
There're copious ways to take you before time
Enviably younger than any exotic game plan!
Professionals are there for target-killing
Silent slow killing is another art of making money
Manifested in diverse ways,
Quite inventively, even when,
Angel-face is conceived as an idea—
—as a foetus in the mother's womb,
Lying as a symbol of the parents' creativity
In the art of procreative genius,
Or possibly even before...

In the murky, messy, cesspool
Keep going straight,
But not curving is too toilsome
But dying is quite a cakewalk:
Plainly drinking the tap water at times might do
We drink non-organic,
'Synthetic milk' of urea and detergents,
Whose branding and patents are wholly owned by us!
We devour juicy, fat, fleshy-tissues
Of the injected, blubbery meat

And death-dealing, waxed
And polished bulging greens
We might die, while driving on roads
Of potholes created by muggers
Freelancing in laundering Black Money into White
And de-laundering White Money into Black!

3

I had a festive chow time in an eating place
At midnight, midway in my deep slumber
My eyes woke up to witness in high fever
Grisly itches pussyfooting over my skin
My heart ached, lungs went shrinking
Stomach got rousing, liver, screeched
Kidney, under strain,
My beefcake was under seizure
An allergic bombardment went in my stomach!

Nerves blew-up on my forehead
I sensed the time might have arrived
For my soul to peep out of me
A gala brunch of yesterday terminated
In a nightmare of food adulteration!
Who'll punish the terrorists
Slow poisoning the guiltless food buffs
While extracting their money?

I had downbeat power to browbeat gripe
But my vocal cord got sunk, down the tubes
The guys who were caught became smart
Greased the palms, unhooking the hooks of law
A decrepit heart wins not against the puissant!
Dying becomes easier many a time
Than living in an unholy-holy or holy unholy land
Hospitals ballyhoo—to be a patient
Having licence to seize and experiment critical organs
In the land of therapeutic, reproductive tourism
Everything costs, has got unfair value!

Super-speciality hawks could perform
Slapdash butchery in the name of surgery!
Fortune is erected on tests and referral
Fake licences might cut organs to dead meat
Making a bloody pulp out of the body
Taking out that extra no-use organ in silence
Leave a piece of surgical equipment as a memento
Body organs are for trafficking to the needier
Those who whistle blowing, might breathe their last
Professionals zero tolerate; call for a blow out
The whistle of the whistle blower blows off!

We do have every right to dream here--
How to die is a super speciality

More options are there, than anywhere, nonetheless
What is guaranteed is only that you'll die
Phenomenally pretty younger, indisputably,
In an inconceivably ingenious modus operandi
In the holy-unholy, homeland of Gods and Goddesses!

A few Reflections:

"If a country is to be corruption free and become a nation of beautiful minds, I strongly feel there are three key societal members who can make a difference. They are the father, the mother, and the teacher."

Dr. A. P. J. Abdul Kalam

*"We smile at each other
And I lean back against the wicker couch
How does it feel to be dead? I say.
You touch my knees with your blue fingers
And when you open your mouth,
A ball of yellow light falls to the floor,
And burns a hole through it."*

Conversation: *Ai*

38

That Benign Smile

That benign smile, is the most wanted
The smile that won the hearts of millions
The smile that fulfilled, need, desires and greed
The smile that poured love out of his heart
While doing selfless deeds till the end!

He made no statue of himself
Nor parks, elephants' statues
No boots, no shoes, only slippers, he had
Bare-chested, in loin cloth
He distributed love in villages!
Trust guarded his chest
He trusted no bulletproof jacket
No black cats, no Z-security but love
He supported himself on walking stick!
He led people, taught by his life, the value of freedom
Made salt out of sea water, challenging the Queen's empire
Where the Sun never set!
When the Father brought the big cake---
Independence---to home

He handed over to his children to enjoy
And went for fasting and 'Satyagraha'
To purify his soul, living for peace, love and compassion!
The people whom he loved,
One put bullets into his heart to silence him
And with him love, truth, justice and nonviolence:
Cremating the principles he gave his life for
And he prayed to forgive the shooter!

Why remember, that saint of a man now?
The phenomenon once walked?
On the earth—Mahatma Gandhi!
But his benign smile is the most wanted
Even now, it is traded on good and fake paper
Pocketed by both enemies,
Enemy countries, followers alike
Delighted in making and faking millions of prints
Of the toothless smile, not out of love,
But more out of love for naked power!
Those warmongers against injustice
Might even betray the trust vested in them
Those 'Trusts' created for a cause
Might tempt them indulging
Many a charitably uncharitable deed!
The most-wanted smile got stained in soiled hands
Circulated, fast beyond the borders, with no trace
In glossy colour prints to grease palms, on the way

Before reaching safely to Swiss chests
Doing and undoing good and bad
Warring for and against good and evil
Does anyone care here anymore?
If 'have-nots' die young, starving and sick
That's because of their laziness to find job!
If some die running after life and suburban trains
That's because of not being smart to move on
Leaders and traders trade money in glee,
Out of the smiles of the saint, honestly selling dishonesty
Advertising, marketing and orchestrating
Money is there to buy not only votes
But organs, flesh, even conscience are on sale!

A few Reflections:

*"O I have been dilatory and dumb,
I should have made my way straight to you long ago;
I should have blabbe'd nothing but you. U should have chanted nothing but You."*
To You: *Walt Whitman*

"He who doubles the revenue eats up the people's property."
"Just as it is not possible to know when the fish moving in water drink water, similarly, it is difficult to find out when officers employed in the execution of works misappropriate money."
Chanakya

39

Farm Land

Debt grew---
In the Farmland:
Dreams dried up;
In drought,
With no harvest!

Those who toiled the farm,
Mixing their sweat, tears and blood,
Went to sleep in the darkness,
After the Last Supper,
Blowing out
The tiny flickering light in them
Never to return to the flame in the farm land!

Their bodies hung on tree tops
Swinging in the air, amidst the green leaves
Looking down over the farms
Overseeing the land, once owned by them
Over-viewing helplessly the land,
That's eaten away,
By land-hungry creditor-sharks!

Will those farmers' souls,
Lost the bodies in the deal,
Hovering now around their corpses,
Find finally solace in the other world,
Not able to pay off their debts in this world?
When their tear-eyed children,
Wail for food, crying out of their empty tummy,
Looking at the bundled up corpses of their hope,
Brought down from the branches of the green trees;
Where're the hands
To feed those weeping children?
Those orphaned kids of malnutrition
Grin at their future, hung in the air swinging
Over their lost, homeless, farmland
Their empty stomachs,
Signify dark, deep, patches of mourning,
On the painted, glistening,
Sexy high cheek bones of beautiful India Inc.!

A few Reflections:

"O God! Can I not save
One from the pitiless wave?
Is all that we see or seem
But a dream within a dream?"
             A Dream Within A Dream: *Edgar Allan Poe*

"Power tends to corrupt, and absolute power corrupts absolutely."
                                         Lord Acton

40

Now You Tell Me

1

You –
Yes, I mean, you
Now, you tell me;
Because, I don't know
When it happened and how?
Because, you're a damn good professional!

Might be, it occurred at midnight
Yesterday—yes, when
The midnight hid its secrecy
In the womb of darkness, rehearsing,
In its criminal mind!

No, I don't know
May be today
Before the Sun got up from of his bed
When Dawn woke up
After the night snooze
Don't ask me, I plead you

I DON'T KNOW
DO YOU UNDERSTAND ME NOW?

But, no doubts should you've,
I do demand from you
Only the right answer
Who did that?
'Cause, you're a damn good professional!

Tell me, now
Am I still somnolent?
Or am I riding a hobbyhorse
Inebriated by liquor or ego or both
Am I dead and gone; or still alive?
I don't know, but you've to inform me
Because, you claim,
You're a damn good professional!

2

It is all about an innocent, twittering fledgling
Just before initiating into life
Dreaming to scale the heights of the sky
Flapping wings, to soar in the air
It is all about a fresh snow dewed baby rose
Eagerly waiting to bloom into a flower

It is all about a virgin thought
Untainted, like a dove's white snowflake feather!

It is all about a feverishly shooting up
A bamboo shoot, hankering to sprout in the sky
You're right, it is all about
A pretty little, school going butterfly teen
A 'wide-eyed princess',
Who weaved many palaces in her dreams
Hiding a few secrets
In the secret locked chamber of her heart
Of sharing her saga
Of bliss with her prince charming!

Her young desires linger
In the altar of her psyche
She saw her life showcasing
In the lime flame of fame
Her fantasies passionately entered
The realm of movie stars
Enacting intriguing hysterics
On the silver screen of her mind
Horizon of her mind expanded
In the information highway
May be indulging, in surrealistic dreams

Shooting before the camera
For many romantic films to be screened!

3

Her deep sea, coffee brown, lively eyes
Silently shining but communicate her dreams
Yes, true, the chick used to try flying
Flapping on its untrained tender wings
Like an angel loves to fly the heights
A Kristen Stewart, shining in Hollywood
A Kareena Kapoor Khan, in Bollywood
Breaking a new dawn in a twilight saga
A dancing star like Lady Gaga
Or Beyoncé Knowles, or Adele
Of 'Skyfall' and 'Rolling in the Deep'
Putting the heart and soul
Inside someone's hand
Playing to the beat and that someone
Could have knifed it, cut into pieces
And thrown it to dogs after use!

She looked like a nymph in a fairy tale
Late-night parties showed her
Eyes drunk in dreams
A show-stopper –
A queen babe in the making---

In the Hollywood of the Bollywood
May be not so holy world!

I knew nothing
More than what I confessed to you
Neither did I seek to know more
Why should I dwell on such unpleasant stuff?
When Bacchus served me liquor
When I was in my own world
Of clubbing, gambling, partying.....
You can say I play golf18 to 36 holes often
But what's the crime in hitting the ball?
Why can't I keep my golf clubs at home?
But I know, you'll find them perfectly unstained!

Didn't I tell you, that night, I got a little dizzy?
In cocktail circuits, afloat in the liquor pool
You find me enjoying orgasmic exuberance
Did the golf club, kept at home
Hit that night so hard...a strange ball?
You doubt, causing the soul of a ball airborne,
Struck hard by a club-head,
So hard to fly it in the infinite sky;
Never to return ever!
I'm absolutely at loss, I don't know
Smoking pot might be
Making clouds over my mind;

Brain forgets to work for a while:
Has gone holidaying, it seems,
I want your explanation,
I repeat, you should tell me, now
Who did it that night and why?

4

I was sleeping with my wife that night
Not with other's wife, anyway
You've a problem?
I cannot help snoring in our bedroom
Only after locking all doors from inside
True, I drank that night with my wife too
You should know, I was weary after work
Do you have a problem?
If I fell in deep slumber, snoring like a boar,
Unaware of anything happened,
After a hectic day, over a few pegs,
A good round of love making,
That too that night only
With my wedlocked partner
But, I confess, I don't know
Did my partner abandon me?
Under the umbrella of darkness at night!
Did she lock or unlock
Any or no room in our house
Don't ask me, I told you, I don't know!

Now, I have a problem
You should confirm
Who killed my daughter?
Who saw the killer?
Throwing her bedroom key
On the floor
When we were sleeping,
Hugging each other in solid slumber?

You're an inspector of crime branch
Find out, that's your goddamn job
Did the killer take Bloody Mary?
Rum, Vodka or Brandy!
You should know whether
He consumed alcohol at all or not
Before or after the crime
And if you say Scotch,
Then how did blood appear
In the Scotch
And on the edge of a glass?

Tell me, you, I mean, you
Tell me now
When I was asleep
Cuddling my wife in love
Did I have a surge of testosterone?
Who entered her room?
To silence the chick in her

Behind the locked bedroom
Of my darling solitary, pretty teen daughter
Who changed the bed sheets, swept the floor
And, you must know
It's quite shocking
I've to tell you, note, please,
They changed her panties too!

Happy I'm to acknowledge
You're a goddamn criminal investigator
But sorry, I can't believe what you say
It could be the wind
Who came through the window
To take the wind out of her
When the drunken darkness
Snored in snooze
Pillowing on the bulging chest
Of his mistress—the murky night
Are you still in a fix?
If my baby lived as wholly mine...
After all, you know,
I've given life to her
May be only her mom might differ
But won't dare to say to anyone the truth
I don't know, let her speak to you
I agree with you,
DNA can speak the truth!

Tell me now,
Am I in dreams?
Am I in delirium?
Am I done, dead and gone?
Or am I still alive?
Now I feel, I'm out of me
I'm fed up of I, Me and Myself peeping out
I'm tired of me, my good self
Am 'I' fading out in 'Me'?
Slipping the 'I' out of the shell of 'Me'---
I'm not 'I' any more, what I used to be
Why I feel more than one soul
Are there many souls popping out of my psyche?
Are there more than one 'I's in 'Me'?

Why am I looking stranger to me?
Is it a sign of Schizophrenia?
Tell me; am I in a mental asylum?
Did anyone overpower 'I' in 'Me'?
Did spirits possess 'I' in 'Me' or what?
Am I a doctor or a patient?
Or am I in a drunken hallucination?
Or in a messy deep paranoia?
Hasn't every man got a conscience?
I hear something deep from me
Making my fingers trembling out of guilt
Can the detergents wash the stains
From my hands under the gloves?

A few Reflections:

"Will all great Neptune's ocean wash this blood from my hand?
No, this my hand will rather the multitudinous seas incarnadine,
Making the green one red"

Macbeth: *Shakespeare*

"Hate the sin, love the sinner."

Mahatma Gandhi

"Only to live, to live and live! Life, whatever it may be!"
"Nothing in this world is harder than speaking the truth, nothing easier than flattery."

Crime and Punishment: *Fyodor Dostoevsky*

41

Tossing Game

1

'Let me bat
Let this be my last game
Then I'll retire';
Announced the batsman!
Ooh! Oops! Ummm....
Bowlers found him
An impenetrable fortress:
Shooting cannons
After cannons in the sky!

His sweeps found sixes,
Boundaries, rolling into tons,
Despite bowlers' googlies;
Throwing ball into left, right and centre
Fielders could only gasp
The hot dusty summer air!

There came a great bowler,
Bowling googlies after googlies!

You, Chinaman!
How do I play, your 'screw ball'?
You, 'Bosey', 'Yorker' 'Doosra'
You tell me, now
Are you throwing?
'The wrong one', 'the other one'
Why do you do it to me?
Bouncing in the pitch spinning,
Breaking down after bouncing,
Spinning to offside,
Why are you making me blind?

I don't see your wrist twisting
Nor do I see you charging
Are you the leg spin-bowler?
Bouncing the ball in the pitch?
Breaking down to my offside?
Bowling by a right arm to offside!

2

When balls went over them
Like catapults in the sky
Showing faces, leaping to catch
Ball bouncing out, tumbling down
Fielders rolled on the meadow!
The bowling team's captain lamented;

"Why did we make hero of that batsman?
He should've been bowled out zero!
I don't know, what's happening!
Oh, Jesus, how do you make our bowlers fail?"

"Guys, you must know, a play is a play;
Like the toss of a coin
Fifty-fifty possibility on either way
Anything could happen and would happen
And should happen, something we desire
Uncertainty is the hallmark of any game;
We're here to make things happen!";
Asserted Bookies out of their experience!

"What's there? Aren't we in the business of fixing!
I mean booking games!
Register and gamble with us, you'll love it
Gambling makes the game exciting
It gives more fun, when money is batting the ball!
In this money-making game, skills are not so important
Neither in batting or bowling or fielding
In the games organised for money!"

Bookies taught them the philosophy of the game;
"When money bats, bowls
Money only calls shots--
Catches, drops in this ball game!

Guys, why wait, join us?
For gala time of gambling the game!
Put your money for bouncing
Spinning, circling, spiralling and
Rebounding going beyond
Boundary and sixes in the games!

This play can also be quick fixing,
Believe us; you'll make money
When we make money
Players are paid to play our game
Not their game or anyone else's game!
Why worry how to play?
We're here to fix it for you!
And we don't fix it anyway,
Someone else will fix them,
Fixing any way will be done!
And gambling is sheer fun,
Like batting in reverse sweep!"

3

Some game lovers pray to God
And the atheists petted the Dogs
Before gambling the game began
Bookies played games
Both for God and Dog lovers

Fixing some, not fixing some
And getting tense,
And feeling easy and great
Getting defeated, and winning off and on!

If the bookies don't play their game
Who'll play their game for them?
Who'll gamble for them, if they won't?
Commentator commented cool
Nobody knew, what they knew
Or not knew--- about the inner game!

The story of the ball is intriguing
Began with test tournaments
Moved on to fifty-fifty; and now
You're the game maker
You can bid for one-dayers and T-20s too!
If you feel exhausted,
Adrenaline rush is not good enough,
We bookies have got steroid
To get you into the form!
Cheer leaders are here to entertain you, anyway
To cheer you to hit a ball of fire!

There comes on You Tube and Twitter
A sex siren, a sweet Twitterati, displaying her cleavage
Throwing off her panties, humming songs of being open

Before the cameras for the cause of new age cricket-lovers;
"Let my panty fly a flag of pride in the breeze; I don't care;
I'm nude for you my cricketers, I pray let India win!"
And she danced baring all and showing, shedding later crocodile tears;
"What shall I do for you guys more now; men, don't' be so impotent, I say!
My nudity went waste, my dear fellows, still you made India lose;
That's what saddens me! Come on guys, if you've fire of passion in you now,
You'll surely win betting, fix the game,
Be nude and shameless and don't forget fixing me too
We're in the lovely company of the ancient Greek Gods –
Naughty Bacchus and sexy Cupid,
Guys you know what we call in India that lusty God Cupid
He's our ancient Indian God of love - Kama Deva!"
Movie stars brawled, terribly losing money
When things went head-down shamelessly naughty!
The rule is simple, when bookies played
Money batted, bowled and went into googlies
In reverse sweep might reach far away in the Swiss banks!
If you like to bid for the batsman

Who says, he would retire?
What a terrific fun in this game is!
Everyone loves, playing money games!
Isn't life too a game?
A bigger gamble played at higher risk?
Game of money is cool indeed
Like the pure aphrodisiac
It fails not invigorating without any age or sex bar!

A few Reflections:

"I am not thinking too far ahead, just want to take it one thing at a time."

Sachin Tendulkar

"I love to play golf, and that's my arena. And you can characterize it and describe it however you want, but I have a love and a passion for getting that ball in the hole and beating those guys."

Tiger Woods

"The one thing you can do for sure, is push the luck on your side."

Roger Federer

"Just play. Have fun. Enjoy."
Michael Jordan

"Success is no accident. It is hardwork, perseverance, learning, studying, sacrifice, and most of all, love of what you are doing or learning to do."
Pele

"A lifetime of training for just ten seconds."
Jesse Owens

"The man who has no imagination has no wings."
Muhammad Ali

"When you lose a couple of times, it makes you realize how difficult it is to win."
Steffi Graf

"Cricket is a game played by 11 fools and watched by 11,000 fools."
George Bernard Shaw

"We are what we repeatedly do; excellence, then, is not an act but a habit."
Aristotle

"Many people say I'm the best women's soccer player in the world. I don't think so. And because of that, someday I just might be."
Mia Hamm

"Winning is a habit. Unfortunately so is losing."
Vince Lombardi Jr

42

The Poisoned Teacher

1

Under the mushroom canopy
Of the elite sky
On the ruins of the Mycenaean Fortress;
At Acropolis in Athens,
On a lofty platform
Raised in the market place
Stood a short stout stocky man
Offspring of a midwife
And a stone-cutter,
The wisest of the buffoons
And the best buffoon among the wisest!

Bulbous eyes
Sat close to the snub-nose,
Staring at people:
A conundrum poked thought-needles,
Mining deep in their mind, drilling brain,
Socrates questioned the Athenians:
What's virtue? What's wisdom?

He did no stone cutting
But did midwifery, like his mother,
But aiding birth of truth and wisdom,
Out of pregnant big belly of confusion!
Didn't he make his wife, not amused
Offering free teaching to the community?

2

Socratic Method made things absorbing
Narrating stories with riddles
Agglomerate did people to listen to stories:
Two men began crossing over a mountain
To a village, on a sweltering sunny day:
A merchant and a man with a donkey!

The merchant hired the donkey,
To carry his merchandise, for the day,
In the blistering midday temperature,
Only one could walk
Under the shadow of the donkey!
And the other man, squabbled interminably,
Saying the shadow belonged to him!

The owner of the donkey altercated,
He had not leased out the shadow,
But the merchant brawled, disputing,

As he had hired the donkey for the day,
The shadow of the animal was his!

Who does own the shadow of the donkey?
Queried the teacher, offering no solution
Crowd got bowled over, not knowing the answer
But the teacher just walked off
Could they chase his philosophy;
'I do not think that I know;
What I do not know!'; he advised;
'By all means marry.
If you get a good wife, you'll become happy;
If you get a bad one, you'll become a philosopher!'
'The unexamined life is not worth living for man'

3

Bizarre were the arguments indeed
Between the two babies in the womb;
"You're junior to me, but I must express
There's no life neither here, nor after birth
Incarcerated are we in this crazy vessel,
Life is entangled in the messy umbilical cord
Will there be any life even after our birth?"

"Oh, brother, life is beautiful wherever we are
It's the mind that brings beauty in life

Joyful will be life always for us
What matters is the way we look at!
Get ready for a great life after birth too!"

"Huh! Ha! Stupidity has limits, but not yours
What sort of jagged life are you day-dreaming?
Hanging yourself tied up inextricably
On this jumbled, umbilical cord in a Hara-Kiri?"

"I don't know, how it would be
But I believe we'll have fine food
Run on our feet, drinking mother's milk
Lots and lots of fun and we can laugh aloud!"

"Dim-witted dull-headed buffoon, aren't you?
Haven't you measured the umbilical cord?
Isn't it damn short, higgledy-piggledy stuff?
Walking and eating by ourselves is just impossible
This nasty navel string can strangulate and kill us both!"

"Brother, don't, please don't ever cut it, it's our life tube
Saving you and me, giving us air, water and food
Let me ask you; my dear wise brother
Have you seen or heard anyone returning
To the womb, he or she left after the birth?

We're here immobile, growing healthy and well
Dropping in the darkness is a way of getting ready
For enjoying a splendid life outside the womb
Our dear mother must be eagerly waiting for us."

"In this lousy jail, I see no mother
The hell will take care of us
How can there be a mother
In this freaking dungeon?"

"Our mother is all around, encircling us,
She is the love that hugs you and me
Keeping us secure, alive, warm and good
We're in her; she is sacrificing everything for us
Touch, this place please; it's our mother
Without mother, how can there be any life?
We wouldn't have existed at all without her care!"

"An atheist I am; believe only truth that I see
Why should I believe things only others see?
I don't understand all that codswallop you're up to!"

"I can touch my mother, I feel our mother
I can hear her singing, I sense how she feels
She is joyful, doing everything possible for us
And we're going to have great life after birth!"

"May be you're getting ready
For death even before birth
I wonder; how a stupid like you can
Be my twin brother?"

"We'll live nicely, my sweet brother
There is going to be good life after birth
Our mom is not going to kill us
We're XY chromosome-Combo children
Boys are not XX chromosome combo
Unlike girls, we're in great demand in this land
We might find life, even after death
In a different world in a different way!"

4

Athens remained the Socrates' classroom
All Athenians were his treasured students
Socratic Method of dialogue probes deep
Knows not the answer, but drills to the bottom
Till knowing, asking right questions
Seeking right answers to the riddle of life!

The teacher provoked the pupil
Like a gadfly, stinging lazy horses to gallop
Dialectics was his tool of knowing the truth!

Plato conceded his abecedary
The wisest and the most just
Best of all men, he had ever known!
The loyal disciple of Socrates,
The greatest thought-provocateur in the world
Authored 'The Republic', taught in the Academy
Law, astronomy and philosophy
Ideas and ideals, and thoughts!

Plato discovers that the chariot of life
Is strung to the three souls—
Sex, aesthetics and pleasure of the mind:
First soul—sex, tied to the chariot is corporeal,
Runs amuck in uninhibited vigour;
Second soul—spirit is mortal, living in the heart,
Third soul—reason tied to the chariot is eternal
That's the brain that steers the chariot,
Controlling the other horses with will power!

Pericles built the 'Golden Age of Greece'
Rebuilt Acropolis and Parthenon,
In the bastion of liberalism and democracy!
Socrates was found not a democrat
Nor was the teacher an egalitarian
Arguing that people shouldn't be self-governing!

Politicians might be rip-off artists
Poets understand not even own poetry
Death is not an issue to be chickened out
When loyalty to what one believes is on test!
Right and wrong may be argued
But acting right or wrong is what matters!

5

The comic poet Eupolis created character
To ridicule the selfless community teacher;
"Yee, I loathe that poverty-stricken windbag
Socrates, who contemplates everything in the world
but does not know, where his next meal is coming from."

When Aristophanes' comedy—"The Clouds"—begins
There appears a comic, eccentric, headmaster
Ambling along the streets of Athens, barefooted
Rolling his eyes, gawking up at the clouds often
That sophist of him is alleged corrupting the young minds
Framing arguments solid to justify beating own father
And teaching the leader of the 'Thirty Tyrants'
Of the ruthless ancient oligarchic regime!
Aristophanes' character enjoys speculating,
Pronounces a key research hypothesis;

'Rain is nothing, but Zeus pee-peeing through a sieve'
There you see he deploys the Socratic elenchus
Doesn't the null hypothesis get eliminated?
Doesn't pure dialectic find nothing; but the truth
A fool proof modus operandi, beyond prejudicial slander!

Diogenes bemoans Socrates brainstorms moral issues,
In an air of superciliousness, men set upon him, with their fists,
Or tore his hair out of his loopy head!
Was he a loveable, mad, vagabond?
Isn't a Damocles' Sword dangling on his head?
Isn't he casting a disquieting shadow of a vulture
Afloat in the air over the people's rule of the city state?

6

Didn't the Oracle of Delphi proclaim
No one was wiser than Socrates?
Socrates wondered; he had no wisdom
Great or small, but God couldn't be lying
Ignoramus could be possibly the most profound!
Could the king clown be the brainiest?
Inconceivable might be concealing wisdom;
"I am the wisest man alive, for I know one thing
And that is I know nothing"

"Men of Athens, I honour and love you;
But I shall obey God rather than you,
And while I have life and strength
I shall never cease
The practice and teaching philosophy"!

The septuagenarian teacher was charged
Of impiety of teaching wrong things
And poisoning the young minds of Athenians!
Non-apologetic was Socrates in his 'Apology'
No grudge had he got against the jury
Wasn't he Plato's Socrates—a hero in 'The Republic'?
Serving three battles as a hoplite
Wasn't he the greatest teacher ever known to humanity?

Three hundred and sixty jurors
Voted for death to him
Socrates bid farewell to his people
The philosopher silenced him, thereafter
Swallowing the law
Drinking hemlock to death!
His was one of the greatest speeches
Ever made in the history of humanity;
"The hour of departure has arrived
And we go our ways-I to die and you to live
Which is the better only God knows."
Scholars argue, it wasn't Socrates' oratory

But his disciple—Plato's eloquence!
Athenians didn't allow
Defendants to speak after sentencing!
Doesn't Socratic elenchus remain valid even now
Pursuing goodness before selfish interests?

A few Reflections:

"The reeds give
way to the
wind and give
the wind away"
        Small Song: *A. R. Ammons*

"Correspondingly, the angelic curls
Grow more blonde, the skin gains its distant, lordly
White, while the bedding already coils
Desperately in the basement laundry."
      Dutch Mistress: *Joseph Brodsky*

"Here's me when we were in Llandudno on our honeymoon.
I painted my toenails red. If you cared to look you could see
I shall have my toenails red. I do this by myself with no help,
And that's me dancing around the house – it was the fresh air
Kept me going, without a single brown penny in my purse."
      Better Life: *Sir Andrew Motion*

43

Of Wolf Men and Wolf Women

1

Seven white wolves
Looking like long-tailed foxes
Sit on a walnut tree
At midnight
In front of my window
Stare at me, growling!

The window frame breaks open
Wolves jump on my bed
In the orgy of their hunger
I befall, getting butchered,
Blood-dribbling, pounding into,
Red meat dollops, pulverizing,
Between the grisly teeth, chewed up,
And nudge into the cave belly,
That hides mammoth hunger-ogre!

An infant sleeps
In his room, all alone
And wakes up, terrified,
Out of the nightmare,
That's the Wolf Man,
Of Freud, the psychoanalyst,
Making the patient
Confessing in hypnotic slumber!

Under the body mountain
Where River-Blood flows
Where lamps light the brain cells
Freud stumbles on, that the Wolf Man
Had witnessed the taboo----
Of his parents having sex
When he was an infant!

When Freud was no more
Doubted seriously the Wolf Man
Wasn't it likely?
Couldn't Freud's analysis be wrong?
Was he cured or wasn't he?
And wasn't Freud obsessed with sex?
Did he also suffer from any syndrome?

2

A glow-worm, flickers
In the darkness of obscurity
Switching on and off reminiscences
Screening the life cinema
On the silver-screen of my mind!

The star-eyed teens fly like butterflies
In the college campus from flower to flower
Some flowers smile at every butterfly
Many a flower burns, green with envy!

A bird of a mountain soul
Perches on the green wood tree
In front of my tree house
Sings a song of dreams to me
Radiating the flame of passion!

The fluttering wings transmit energy
The twirls of desires
Sprinkled in fragrance, in the yellow light,
Germinate gold, in reverie!

The feathers of a rainbow, dressed like,
A cockatoo girl, she is;

Playing Beethoven's Ninth Symphony,
On the strings of my heart-piano!
The ice breaks at the bar
Beer drops spill over the glass
Drips in the mouth of the hungry dragon
Encircling the pierced belly button
Focussed only in eating own tail;
'Let your dragon gulp a drop of beer too
It might add taste while swallowing its tail';
I humoured.
That black tattooed Ouroboros dragon
Curling on her fair belly
Will never finish consuming its tail
Possibly till the end of the universe!'

The macaw bird tweeted;
'Being young, I'm fresh,
But, not experienced;
I've got confused,
I landed up as a lesbian!'
'Not a problem!'; said he;
'I had my stint too, as a gay
Let us go partying, let us date;
Let us make things happen!'
She was my Phoenix girl
The fire of my passion
Resurrecting often

Like the legendary bird of fire
Blazing out of ashes, singing the fire song!
The first sparkle of love
Lights the heart in flame:
'You're no longer a village idiot
But a metro-heterosexual man
You look like a painter, come on
Brush me raw, into colours'
Canvas cuddled voluptuousness
Coloured in nude, portraying
The lyrics of desire with acrylics!

We did what we loved to do
On the canvas, brush-stroking feelings
In the ecstasy-fire, in search of the mystery
Hidden in the folded follicles—
—The symbolic geometry of life
Gazes at me, creating a magnum opus—
—A Red Flower on Fire
My first nude in lyrical abstract expressionism!

Your words echoed and re-echoed
In the valley of the mind;
'I want, not just you
I want everything of you
Absolutely full of my man
You; I' can't share with anyone!'

3

A child of originality,
A fair girl, savoir-faire,
Full of oomph at every touch of innocence
Researching new ways of kissing the original;
'I'm denuding, only for the original portraits
Not just my body, but my emotions too
Can you absorb me full?
Hug me, like a live teddy bear
Be an Adam of a man to your Eve!
Enjoy savouring a ripened red apple
Haven't you noticed pentagram
Crisscrossing the forbidden fruit?
I can be too spicy and gaga in heat
Make only my original portraits—
The imprints of sensuality,
Impregnated in the curves'

'An exquisite piece of art, you're
A serpent girl of love, invaluable
Unique, not just your thumb impression
But the design, those chiselled organs
Every note of the composition of the music,
Every flavour, fervour, of the fruit,
The invigorating scent of the night flower,
Folding flesh and raising mounts are beguiling!

I'm a hum-drum painter, though,
But you made the difference,
Pouring passion in my paintings,
Expressing in colours man's hollow nakedness;
In red, blue, pink, purple, golden yellow!

Money came rolling
By selling the abstract lyrical nudity,
And still life nudes in cubism,
And you groomed me a painter,
Specialising in nude portraits, avant-garde,
And we could've settled down in life, then;
Just sharing moments of love and fun'!

4

In the art galleries, exhibitions conjured up
Billionaire connoisseurs of art fancied nudity in colours
Feral, feminine, carnal desire on fire
Fantasising the one impishly libidinous,
I didn't know, how things would curve down then;
But I knew, your magic appeal,
When the billionaire owned all your portraits
Exhibited at Lambert Yvon Galerie in Paris
And left no coloured nudity unsold in the gallery
Even the blonde, kissed and tanned by hot sun!
The billionaire showed so much allure

For the collector's naked pieces!
What a party to follow the grand sale
Blondes, brunettes, redheads
Curly, straight, silky, painted hair
Ballroom dancing with the connoisseurs!
Time of cheers for cheers and by cheers
Springs up, when loosened cork of joy, opens up
Champagne overflows in laughter,
Bursting into a fountain of joy in the air
Ejaculating the vigour, sweetened in aroma!

'Hey, master portrait maker
How do you find this lovely painting?
I want this beauty of a portrait too
To be the most priced collection—
Like a Mona Lisa alive
In the museum, called my bedroom
Yes, this multi-dimensional one
Only this pulchritudinous butterfly,
Can possibly elevate my sagging spirits,
To the seventh heaven of bliss—Nirvana!
Money is nothing! Poor is money
I pity money, before the goddess of love
I'll own this Aphrodite, for, I wish to be her Adonis!'

There he was the king of money,
The worshipper of beauty

Owning my best art piece of love
I'm sure she'll emerge the winner
In any beauty pageantry
Like in 'El Judicio de Paris'
Among the best of the beauties
Bathing in the spring of Mount Ida!

That was the only one painting
I would have never sold,
To anyone in my whole life
But, I lost it to him not for money
Because he had more than money
To own anything his eyes fancied!

I saw the serpent girl giggling
Passion snaking along the billionaire tree
In a bear enfoldment, locking his lips in hers
Into silence, absorbing nectar in bliss!
You flew away scaling new heights
In the limitless open sky
Leaving your pair bird in melancholy
Looking in despair at the distant sky
Praying the cockatoo love bird to return.

Rejection bladed my heart into slits
I felt spiralling on my own axis
Fainting in oblivion; and,

Encircling around the axis of the lost dream,
Waking me up in nightmare!

'Lost love gives high fever
The fiery fire of betrayal
Consumes you from within
You need to denude your soul
Love needs taking off layers
Outfits of hypocrisy and lies'!
The inquisitive lady psychiatrist
Undressed my emotions, exploring me
In hypnotic slumber
Inner complexities revolving around
The aroma of the body crevices
Sweaty, salty, sour, raw, tastes of lust
Illusions, bashed up fantasies
Crushed desires turning into syndromes
Insomnia continued with intermittent
Nightmares and spell of hallucinations!

'Undulating highs and lows
Of the waves of emotions
Don't you've a problem?
An abrasion of intimacy
An abnormal opus humming
In your ears, playing on your nerves
Shooting in you, debilitating pain—

A feeling of chronic emptiness
A monster baby growing in you, bursting in you
Didn't a spy enter in your house of love?'

The song that merges,
Not in oeuvre
Shrivels, falling down
Like a forgotten petal
Of a faded flower of memory!
The dry leaves from the dream tree
Flow in the rivulets of thoughts
Fades memory, in the academe
Comes alive on my Facebook
As a friend of a friend of a friend
A singing parrot of ideas, chirruping
Through my iPhone
That teenage macaw bird
Metamorphoses into
The celebrity rock star now
Sings beautiful songs
Hauntingly caressing my soul

If you want to be an addict
Be so, by all means:
But be that of pure love
But, you've become an addict of lust

An order becomes a disorder
You've become a Wolf Man!

5

Hey, they're clingy, like puppies
Smooching, pecking and cooing
Like doves.
Many of their slobbery kisses
Share strawberry ice-cream!'

'Oh, my baby, you're suffering
How can I help you?
Where did you find the chap?';
Mom finds her daughter,
Caught in Puppy Love Syndrome!

'Oh Mom, isn't he cute?
I got him with angelic wings
He comes to my Facebook often
I put him as my mascot
On my window screen
Fully muscled for me to see him full
Like the statue of David of Michaelangelo!'

'Great, but baby, did he ever
Reveal his thoughts to you?'

'Mom, we feel, bosom close.
Too much time spent in love
Becomes too little for us
Our equation should work
We'll show you how it does
We're in First Love Syndrome';
She corrects her counselling mother
'I know, you could be right
Nay, don't tell me more, my sweet pie
I'm better off knowing less, for;
Knowing more, might pain my heart
Living in oblivion is bliss, at times ';
Says mom to her daughter!

Delusions turn into honeybees
Dreams weave nest for the birds
She said to her David bluntly:
'May be, I'm self-centred,
An absolute Narcissist, insecure,
Out of control, a hard nut to crack
And love money a lot
But, if you can't help me,
When I'm at my worst,
You deserve me, not;
And when no love clicks
It's time for us,
To depart and move on!'

6

In the business of emotions
Love bundles a combo often
A Cauldron and Pole
The couple become lovers!
In the business of love
Man becomes an addict
Not of money
But of love!

In the love of business
The woman became an addict
Not of love
But of money!

Green budding leaves
Of the Tree of Love
Spread irresistible aroma
A new-fangled perfume
Launches in the air
Flavoured in trendy style
But, the couple, accustomed
Only to classic old scent
Ask; 'what does the rule book say?'
Am I forbidden to have nostrils?
To breathe new pristine fragrance anymore!'

His heart was filled with feelings for her; said he;
'I'll gift you, the best home in the world
On your birthday
You'll cut the cake at your home
On the B' Day Party
Arriving by the air craft I gifted to you
How does it sound to your musical ears?'

'Are you serious?'
'Of course; I'm!
The best songs are those never sung
But you can still listen to the tune
If you fine tune your ears'
'What do you mean?'
'I mean dream and reality
Not differ in intensity of joy!'

'I don't understand you!'
'Castles in the air are fresh in design'!
'I don't want to hear!
Aren't you a billionaire?'
'Did I say so?
Possibly, I can be,
I'm fighting a case in the court;
Though that idea came,
Too late in my mind!
But I'm, truly,

A billionaire, at heart'
'Shut up, you're a fraud;
You lied to me!
I can't love a Nutty Fraud-Liar!'

In the business of life,
She incriminates him
Having a psychological aberration
A maniac of a pie in the sky!

He re-criminates her,
In blistering fire of vindictiveness;
'You do business with the rich males
For the lust and greed for money!'

She runs out of him,
Carrying her passport
And runs into a trader,
Transacting old emotions
Seldom does he believe in them!

He loves using her
Like a love machine for money
Paying even for her shopaholic habits;
'You're soft like a flower
But, I'm a machine of love
Not made of feelings

I want you to adjust
The strings of your life-guitar
Or else, transform me like you a flower?'

7

Some psychics act like boyfriends
Bash up love with iron rod,
And inhumanly insert screw driver
In the red flower of womanhood
Who'll treat those schizophrenic?
Allow not, fiddling with life's soft white,
Petals of innocence to wither away,
In the cruellest tomfoolery of a psycho!

A loop in the brain
Clouds of sorrow cast shadows
Burst into tears over the dark patches
Flow down on the cheeks of sorrow
From the disconsolate eyes!

Nightmare conflagrates in fire storm
Many clouds burst in lightning
Thunder showers at home
Inner emptiness grows in humidity
Smells like fungus
And loneliness thickens its long shadows
Escorting wherever you go!

Isn't he carrying on with a new affair?
Hasn't she entrapped helplessly
In a battered relationship
Love is getting beaten up
Enslaving, convulsing in insecurity
Breaking up the invisible locks of trust
Relationship quivers in pain
Hearts are hit by fire
In thunderstorm and lightning!

The pink petals of reverie
Un-smelt virgin scents of lost love
Un-imbibed chalice filled in wine
Neglected flower of life, full of nectar
The holy grail with tinges of fresh drops
Of life blood oozing, getting wasted!

Helpless prisoners of emotions
In the love's concentration camp
Bundles of cash, marketed emotions
Corpse of moments, stinking as not cremated
Heart lands in the tear-lake, plummeting!

8

You lied to me,
When you came into my life

I heard your songs, coy like a lotus,
Waiting for blooming full
In the cuddling rays of the Sun
Frolicked by a schizophrenic, I didn't know then
Whose syndrome, I'm afraid,
No psychiatrist would be able to diagnose now
Freud died and Jung too died, not hypnotising you;
And you've made me an incurable patient of love!

I remember how all it began
That wintery night, I saw you first time
A stranger to my world of fantasia
I was under a warm shower
Dancing with the man who loved me
Researching diverse dance steps
Known and unknown, inventing, re-creating
New Salsa, ballroom tango, rumba
Tap, waltz, bop, foxtrot, ballet
Mixing styles, stitching together
Aligning our marriage in tune
In the music and rhythm of passion!
Why did you ring our home bell?
Why didn't I send my husband?
Instead of coming down
To see who was at the door!
Like a whirlwind, I stepped down
In a hurry to join back him in the shower

But that lady killer smile you rendered
When I unbolted the door
You stole me in the hurry burry hassle

It was too tough for the bath robe
To cling on an absent-minded me
And it slipped off, showing my innocence
Un-hiding the real me before you
You must be a thief of a blacksmith
You know smart-keying in anybody's locks!

I vouchsafe, I didn't want that way
But what could I do?
I saw your powerful arms lifting me in the air
My heart quivered for a while
Like a dove caught by the hunter

I knew, I was devouring the Satan's apple
In the Garden of Eve
It could have caused a Tsunami in my life
You saved me,
Advising me to be cool like a cat
Creating a safe space for you in me doing our business
To come in my life, duping the man in marriage
A secret I left safe in the labyrinthine
Follicles of the female mystery!

9

A psychopath you're,
Addicted to sex
A maniac you're
Indulging in mechanics of love
Deprived of genuine feelings
Of heart and soul
Indulging in addiction,
Bestiality, twosome, threesome,
Multiple orgy games; lost in size, shape,
Colour, length, depth syndromes and what not?
Who'll teach you that the nudity of soul
Is what nurtures true love to grow,
More than skin nudity, and voluptuousness!
It's tough to erase you from my memory
A sort of mania is what I am suffering now
I can't let you go; nor can I pardon you!
You're the one I fell for,
Putting emotions in my profession
Acting like crazy lovers
We got in the commerce of lust
While making money
Being used as machine of love!
You made me a psychic patient
Causing psychological affliction in me

When my husband asked
Whether I enjoyed sleeping with him
I said boldly, he snored like a pig
And I threw the pig to the other room
You fornicated with me the way I wanted!

I made my wedded man guilty
Shouted him to see a therapist
To cure his embarrassing syndrome
I cut the chain that locked me with him:
'I get no 'O 'with penniless, snoring village swine
You're mummy's son,
Bundled up in Oedipus complex
I'm an ardent daddy's baby—
Though I don't suffer any Electra complex
Good for you, man, to get over the complex
And learn to do a man's wifely duties intensely
Putting soul into the act, not act in to the head
There's rhythm and tune even in nature's music
Listen to the gushing rivulets
In the craggy mountain groin
Practise the cuckoo's song like soliloquy!'
That was the day my husband lost
His wife to his new neighbour, as you advised me.

10

You didn't hear the scream of the bird
Killed in the orgy of Wolf Men
On the streets of rape, molestation
And homicide of womanhood
By a few animalistic, cannibals of men,
Gang raping the consciousness of humanity!

You could justify, there're serial killers,
Psychopaths, worse than, in Hollywood films,
On the streets, murdering womanhood
Stabbing and nailing on the flower of life,
Condemned to offer theirs for a living,
In the unjust patriarchy, created by men!

I don't know how and why
You put my soul in the game of lust?
There you're,
Clever, psychopath of a man
You know how to crush the petals of a woman
Deflowering, and taking the nectar out of her
You, never should I ever forgive?

The life of torture you gave me
Indeed your seed, distended in me

Though you alleged;
My egg joined an alien sperm
That thought bled me anaemic
And you ruined mercilessly our seed!

I shall never forget nor shall I forgive you
You're the thought that consumes me from within
Since the day you lighted fire in all my organs
Pumping overdosing hormones in my blood stream!

You got me branded a Wolf Woman now
An addict of love and lust, a sex maniac
The psychiatrist has got the licence
And you put me in the psychiatric ward
You can have fun with other women
I am an incurable patient of your satanic sins
Your abusive relationship bundles me up
And messing with me, beyond recovery
I wish I could be a Van Gouge or Picasso
To put my impression of you in colours!

You've made me a crumbled crystal memoria
Enclosed in a gorgeous packaging
I cannot get over, but I've to move on,
I say, let it be over, I've to go for partying
Let me have a break, after puffing you off
In a few clouds of dark cigar smoke

And chewing you like betel leaves
And spitting you off out of my system!
I know, I've landed up in psychiatric ward
You abused me, raping our relationship
Molested morals, crucified my life,
My heart is bleeding in the cage
Still, I've to love you, my master abuser!

"You've to be treated; I'm your therapist—
Your Freud?" said your paid psychiatrist;
"Sobbing despair mixes up in insatiated lust
Mind revolves in concentric circles
Your desire ripens into a syndrome
You've become an incorrigible Wolf Woman
Falling compulsively in love and get dejected,
You're suffering from Stockholm syndrome!"
I know his talk therapy cannot cure me
I warn you, If I ever come out of the asylum alive,
That'll be the end of your story
Get prepared for Nirvana, you, my molester!

11

The addict of love fails in love
Seeks true love in the asylum
Discarded by the loveless world

She said: 'Dying in love is sweeter
Than living in a loveless life!'
Like a rose petal, we may flow
Vanish into the abyss of time
When did we last hear the chiming
Of love-bells at the altar of heart last time?
When did LOVE breathe in us last?
When did LOVE bid us goodbye?
Love is the thought, if we kiss,
That makes us immortal!

Like an ardent Tantric devotee
Worship the goddess of love
Bathing her in pure waters of love
Sprinkling perfumes of love
Garlanding her in flowers of love
Anointing in celestial emulsion
Let she be your Venus, the Goddess of Love
You be transformed into the idea of love!

A few Reflections:

"The great question that has never been answered, and which I have not yet been able to answer, despite my thirty years of research into the feminine soul, is 'What does a woman want?'

Sigmund Freud

Every form of addiction is bad, no matter whether the narcotic be alcohol or morphine or idealism.'
Carl Jung

"*The factory siren tells workers time to go home tells them the evening has begun.*
When living with the tall man
Whom I didn't love, I would wander
The streets, dreaming of Italy."
Summer Nights: Deborah Ager

"*I know what you miss*
sings this lake. Car horns groaning
in rush hour. Sweet coffee. Wind
pounding like hammers. Warmth of a lover.
Crickets humming love songs to the street."
The Lake: Deborah Ager

"*I shall lie alone at last,*
Clear of the stream that ran so fast,
And feel the flower roots in my hair,
And in my hands the roots of trees;
Myself wrapt in the ungrudging peace
That leaves no pain uncovered anywhere."
The Last Betrayal: Edith Nesbit

44

A Dimple on the Earth's Cheek

Gravity probe proves
A dimple on the earth's cheeks----
Space time curve
On her face:
Smitten by the black hole!
Einstein was right;
There is space-time whirlpool.

A benign wet face –
A few drops of tears,
Drizzling out of melting,
Shadows of crystallised anguish,
Suspended, quite often,
For sleep walking in the air!
Habitually unsung feelings,
Not shared, hallucinate,
And might loom
In frightening nightmares,
Begotten by sweet dreams!

Many a smile, blooming
In between the thick lips
Might be sensuous to be kissed
But is crushed in biting
In between the teeth in sorrow!
The painter who painted the expression
The feelings on her face, and;
Those accumulated emotions,
As a rainbow, should be admired!

He who chose those vibrant colours
To rub on her sobbing cheeks
Should be her true friend!
Out of the blue, there comes,
A thunderstorm, curving on,
The edge of the dimple,
Infatuated by the spinning black hole,
Orbiting secretly
Around another black hole!

There are black holes and black holes
Sucking energy from wherever they find
Encircling, eating one another
Terrifying, multiplying, growing
Drilling deep down in the mind-mines!
Those warring moments of do before die acts

Of those innocent lives thrown in the open air
Mercilessly out of the moving flights!

The souls of their desires buried alive
In the bottom of the pyramid
Look heaven above, not rehabilitated,
Living the life of animals,
Starving while fighting for mercy,
Warring many food battles, like street dogs!
Earth waits wobbling and quivering
By now, she has waited
For quite a while, patiently,
For Godot to save her,
From the intimidating, impending apocalypse!
Do you believe— this is the way the world ends?

A few Reflections:

"For Thine is the kingdom
For Thine is
Life is
For Thine is the
This is the way the world ends
This is the way world ends
This is the way the world ends
Not with a bang but a whimper."
                    The Hollow Men: *T. S. Eliot*

45

Anacondas in the Sky

Beneath the thundering
Sound of the hooves
Of the stallions racing
On the roof of the sky
Volcanoes burst,
Disgorge fire into space!

Fire rains,
Fire-tornados blast!
Molten fire flows into rivers,
Dispersing life into lava!

A new Bubonic plague breaks out,
Epidemics chew away
Many hearts
In moments!

Earth splits into bottomless pits
Whose keys nobody keeps --

Ooh! Moving trains, dashing in speed,
But falling into abysmal depths!

Those travelling thoughts
In bullet trains,
Flying ideas,
In supersonic aeroplanes,
Sailing weaponry,
In warships and submarines,
Launched emotions in satellites
Crash in the same speed!

2

The aged Mayan calendar
Might be old enough
To die
Time's legs
Might be crippled
NASA's discovery—the solar spot—
A big hole in the magnetosphere
Might bring mortal radiation on earth!

Earlier than the Antichrist
Bombs the globe,
Fire-tornados
Kite-fly anacondas in the sky,

Uprooted roots
Of the redwood trees float,
Into the liquid fire River Amazon,
Tsunamis tear bodies apart;
Oceans scaling up to the hill tops:
Let us run to the highest mountains:
But, why do the mountains
Descend the hills
Sliding downwards, drowning,
Sinking and melting
And merging down into the ocean?

3

Apocalypse be round the corner
Nostradamus be right again
The promulgators of the Rapture
And the Aquarius people
Red hot Planet X—'Nibiru'
Might arrive for the second time
Sixty-five million years after,
To gift earth;
A parting, last kiss, to remember,
Like his first noxious, smooch,
That flushed out the dinosaurs,
Earth might quiver in fever;
Fire-tornados enjoy obliteration!

Red blob Nibiru
Might hide behind the sun globe,
Causing the fire globe
Slipping out of the screws
Of the sky ceiling
Crumbling down, and,
In cascading inferno
Showering and flowing into
The Ocean of Fire,
Eating hungry,
Those shot down stars and moons!

The Judgment Day
Might happen or not;
The mother of all wars on earth –
The war of the Armageddon
Might be fought or not
Ahead of the second coming of the Christ
And the rise of second sun,
Who's the hero of the stars,
Courageous to fight and end the evil,
Beginning of a dawn of peace,
Creating a new Garden of Eden
Harvesting smiles of love and care,
Sowing green bushes,
Of liberty, justice, equity,

What matters is a life—
Joy till the last moment---
The glow of the Candle of Life
In the living moments!

A few Reflections:

"From the calm morning, the end will come
When of the dancing horse
the number of circles will be 9"

Nostradamus

"And I will show wonders in the heavens and in the Earth:
blood and fire and pillars of smoke.
the Sun shall be turned into darkness,
and the moon into blood,
before the coming great and awesome Day of the Lord,
and it shall come to pass
that whoever calls on the Name of the LORD
Shall be saved"

Joel 2:30-32

46

The Story of the Fury

My son Newton told you
Every action has a reaction
You're still on my nerves
Playing wild games on me
Jumping, rocking, and dancing!
It's paining me, beyond the limits
Let me stretch, let me breathe
Let me smile, let me sleep, let me cry
Let me have some space to live
For you, my dear children, only for you!
You stopped still not
Now, you'll bear my reaction
Mother's patience has limits too
Now, I'm stretching out
I've to inhale and exhale to live
I may get wild hiccups at times!

Earth quivered in quakes
Steamed up fury burst out in flow
Water torrents encircled in whirlpools
Mountain Tsunami roared over the coast

Monster after monster ran after life
Mounting fury engulfed, crunching all
Blistering fury spewed out fire
Blazing fire wedded roaring wind
Blasted in fire all that came their way!
Lethal clouds hovered over
Like hungry eagles angling for the kill
Live and dead bodies enmeshed, afloat;
Debris decayed kept its mouth shut
But, silence of death spoke aloud
Live life, but let her live her life too!

A few Reflections:

"Some say the world will end in fire,
Some say in ice.
From what I've tasted of desire
I hold with those who favour fire,
I think I know enough of hate
To say that for destruction ice
Is also great
And would suffice."
        Fire and Ice: *Robert Frost*

"Death be not proud, though some have called thee"
Mighty and dreadful, for, thou art not so,
..
One short sleep past, we wake eternally,
And death shall be no more; death, though shall die."
      Death be not Proud: *John Donne*

47

Baby of Hope

An ogre woke up
At midnight in frenzy
Off the cavernous bottom
Of the ocean floor
Rode over rolling energy torrents
Roaring over the seashore
Scampering in a hunting spree!

It hounded people, uprooted the lives
Squeezing soul out of bodies
Ripping organs in a splash
Shuffling bodies in bloodied mess on the beach
Muddled in mud, enmeshed in wreckage,
Of the crumbled skeletons,
Of compressed edifices,
Scattered all over,
All along the ghostly sea shore!

Lives drained out of the body
Missing, buried alive and crippled:

Amputated body parts, organs
Slept quiet; unable to speak the tragic end!

Clouds of smoke
Puffed out by nuclear reactors
Spread toxic fumes
In the borderless sky
Coughed out gases,
Noxious fumes,
Flitted around over the sea shore
Water sprinklers drenched
The fuming radiators
Watering down
The fury of the fiery reactors
Washing down danger
Along the sea shoreline!

Rescue men believed
In deep-rooted hope
Searching for people, who survived?
Dug deep
In the flotsam and jetsam,
Buried down
In the smashed up bits and bobs
A baby of hope
Screamed then in pain
The wrapped up tiny life

In the coverlet
Cried aloud
In the chilled winter
For mother's milk!

In the buried heaps
Of the corpses of hopelessness
There came alive—a light of hope—
A budding green tender leaf of life
Giving hope, a new dimension of life
In the hopeless ghostly Fukushima beaches
Where ghosts sauntered after the bodies
In the buried city!

A few Reflections:

"Though they go mad, they shall be sane.
Though they sink through sea, they shall rise again.
Though lovers be lost, love shall not,
And death shall have no dominion."
          Dylan Thomas

"Let your light so shine before men, that they may see your good works..."
        The Bible: *Jesus;* Matthew 5:16

48

The Holy Dip for Salvation

What the pilgrims seek is a holy dip
At Mahakumbh Mela---'The pitcher festival'
The largest human congregation on earth!
There, in the waters,
At the confluence of the rivers
Ganga, Yamuna, and mythical Saraswati
At Allahabad in India:
Gods dribbled a few drops of nectar
From the heavenly abode
That can elevate humans to immortal!

The pilgrims rush since then for a holy dip
In holy waters, at holy places, on a holy day
At a holy time of planetary position
Seeking the Elixir of Life!
Are those who go for pilgrimage?
Ready for a real ablution
Not denuding the body alone
But churning of the mind and soul
To cleanse sins that accumulate,

Fighting out battles of good versus evil
To enjoy the nectar of immortality—
The quintessence of human values!

In the washing of sins ceremony
Abandoned are the old and the weak,
Safely at the hands of Gods;
As children get busy chasing after their life,
Leaving parents in the quest for salvation
To take holy souls to heaven above,
For an eternal sojourn free of sins
In a joie de vivre beyond earthly life!
To wash out stained thoughts,
Blemished by evil desires
Saintly men come there for help
Doctored in selfless care
Unbundling bundles of soiled dreams
Holy men washed dirty minds
Purified by disquiet
Rinsing in crucified egocentricity
Plunging in waters of moral filaments!

Bursting in clouds, falling in raindrops
Icing into glaciers, melting in warming
Flowing in rivulets, waving in oceans
Absorbing the grime, purifying the body
It is water that quenches the human thirst!

Do the people crave for a holy dip
Keep the life waters clean?
Do we keep the life-waters clean?
Not throwing the precipitants
Of unending human greed in them!
Do we sustain the water bodies alive?
To absorb the sins of humanity
Lest the rivers die of human misdeeds
Incapable of preserving life on earth!

Immortality is, what takes the humans,
Beyond mortality; what we leave when
We're no more is what makes life worthwhile!
Leaving immortal is the Elixir of Life;
Sublime humane deeds, words, and thoughts
Live beyond the confines of the body!

A few Reflections:

"When old age shall this generation waste,
Though shalt remain, in midst of other woe
Than ours, a friend to man, to whom thou say'st,
'Beauty is truth, truth beauty,--that is all
Ye know on earth, and all ye need to know"
                    Ode on a Grecian Urn: *John Keats*

49

Hunting Strategy

He was asked to hunt
Finding out a winning strategy
Like a cheetah, grabbing its prey
Bringing risk to the minimum!
But, cheetah knows how to climb on the tree
For a conscious nap
Meditating on the opportunity to arrive!
Grazing down below the tree, in ease
The eyes are focussed, overseeing
Dreaming about the prey
To be squeezed under its jaw
To be made immobile in its clutching claws
Pounding for the fatal scrabble
To be constricted in its jowl—ripped open
Blood dripping in its dagger fangs
And safely goes in its hungry belly!

In strategy hunting
The greenhorn knows not
Where to look for the opportunity

But sees only an angry tiger
Couched on a chair,
Grumpy, grouchy, snarling
Exhibiting its razor-sharp incisors!
First, the greenhorn felt its claw
Piercing deep into the soul
Blood spilling, bones crushing, flesh tearing apart;
'You're fired'; said the tiger of a boss.
The greenhorn knew
The strategy hunting is not that cool
Before the tiger kills you
You, becoming its food
Fight and kill the beast
By becoming more powerful
Before the beast slaughters you!

A few Reflections:

'...Bliss is not something to be got.
On the other hand you are always Bliss.
This desire (for Bliss) is born of the sense of incompleteness.
To whom is this sense of incompleteness?
Enquire. In deep sleep you were blissful.
Now you are not so.
What has interposed between that Bliss and this non-bliss?
It is ego.
Seek its source and find you are Bliss."
                                        Bliss: *Ramana Maharshi*

"In this part of the story I am the one who
Dies, the only one, and I will die of love because I love you.
Because I love you. Love, in fire and blood."

I Do Not Love You: Pablo Neruda

"There's no knowledge without right faith,
No conduct is possible without knowledge,
Without conduct, there's no liberation,
And without liberation, no deliverance."

Jaina Sutra: Mahavira

"Don't walk behind me; I may not lead. Don't walk in front of me; I may not follow. Just walk beside me and be my friend."

Albert Camus

"Two things are infinite; the universe and human stupidity; and I'm not sure about the universe."

Albert Einstein

"A real 'karma-yogi', who first acquires knowledge and then works for the welfare of people, quite naturally becomes popular and famous. There is no enemy of such a man but even there are, he is able to vanquish them. His popularity in the society increases on account of his successes and good deeds."

Sama Veda

50

Idea Chicks

Egg of an ostrich is big
Huge, elliptical, hard-shelled
But brittle—
Find them hidden
In the arid landscapes
Of the mindscape!

Fetch them—
Those eggs need to be hatched—
With care, wild as they are:
A few, new chicks may come out
Breaking the shells
Pecking in the sunlight
In the valley of vision!

Idea might pour out of confusion
Like light striking in the cloudbursts
Enemies of new ideas might conspire
Prowling eagles might snatch away chicks!

Keep the eggs in the basket of the mind
Away from the thieves, eyeing on them
Giving own body temperature
To hatch them, the idea coming out
Shield the chicks from the thieves
Soaring around shadowing like eagles
Or like foxes and indecent wild cats!

Idea chicks are too tempting to resist
For swooping on and lifting the chicks
Even if hidden in heaps of thoughts
Safely covered in the basket of your mind!

Let lots and lots of eggs of ideas be hatched
Ideas mate ideas, breeding innovative ideas
Let innovative ideas breed fresher thoughts
Multiplying solutions to human problems!

A few Reflections:

"I want to put a ding in the universe."
                                    Steve Jobs

"It's fine to celebrate success but it is more important to heed the lessons of failure."
                                    Bill Gates

"By giving people the power to share, we're making the world more transparent."
                                    Mark Zuckerberg

51

Mind Tree

When dreams
Flower in mind tree
Wait for a while
For the fruits to come
Fruits of the bathed imaginings
Taste sweeter,
If dipped in wisdom!

While picking up
Packaged idea fruits
Sold in the bazaar,
Be cautious
You may find them,
Teeming in venomous fumes
Be sure,
There's no carnage of trust,
Doing away with mankind;
No bombing of budding desires!

Incarcerate those hawkers,
Who sell fruits of ideas—
Those kiss virus into the mouth
Decipher those codes,
Arrest those ideas
Send those thoughts
To the slaughter house
And hammer the last nail
On their coffins!

Like a woodpecker,
You may like to peck
The deadwood of the mind tree
Taking out the rotten cells
In the brain tree
Flushing out the seeds of germs --
Replacing the cobwebs
Of the infected chip
That chipped in
With a new brain chip—
A branded new software
Whose source code
Is known to you!

Those guys
Who store ammunition
In their mind

Wait not,
To explode
That programme in time;
They run after lives wild for a while
Like mountain rats,
Though chased by cats:
Ransacking cities,
Bombing lives,
Burning homes
Raping women,
Abducting children,
Massacring people!

Before letting their dangerous dreams
Flower into fruits and seeds
Bomb their mind into flames
Before bursting lives into fire
Refill their minds
With seeds of love for mankind!

A few Reflections:

*"You will hear thunder and remember me,
And think: she wanted storms. The rim
Of the sky will be the colour of hard crimson,
And your heart, as it was then, will be on fire."*
         You Will Hear Thunder: *Anna Akhmatova*

52

Worms of Ideas

Deep down,
Dumped in the sea bed,
A dead-body of worms of ideas
Wrapped in a bundle,
With weights attached to it,
Never to surface again,
To be devoured by sharks!

Those venomous worms of ideas,
Infect young minds growing virus,
Uprooting dreams,
Spreading kernels of odium!
Those weeds massacre hopes,
Trade hatred, kill hope, purity in thoughts!

They enjoy feeding bombs,
To the hungry mouths,
Of the innocent multitudes,
And rupture sacred sanctum sanctorum
Of the pristine temple of mind!

In a vale of sorrow, in a land
Where hope gets butchered
Mind is inflicted by the mire of infections
And possessed by evil spirits
Sowing and planting seeds
Of devilish ideology
Of not allowing others to live
On the planet earth in love and peace
There is no way out,
But bombing the ghosts
Blowing out the evils, evacuating
The young minds of weeds of ideas
And sowing new seeds of ideas
To bloom into fresh flowers and fruits!

It is time to enliven the human spirit
That has been bedridden,
In the ICU to help to walk out hale and hearty
For creating a brave new world
Where there is abundance
Of fresh oxygen of life and golden rays of hope
A brighter new sky
With new Sun, Moon and Stars!

Begin fishing fresh ideas like a polar bear
Patiently looking in the glacier waters

Waiting for the fish to jump into its mouth
Look for the new idea to arise in the horizon
A brave new global village for everyone to live
With no fear of terror, re-discovering true love!

A few Reflections:

*"That corpse you planted last year in your garden,
Has it begun to sprout? Will it bloom this year?
Or has the sudden frost disturbed its bed?"*
  'The Burial of the Dead'; Waste Land: *T. S. Eliot*

*"Obama meets Osama
Brandishing a word
As deadly as the sunlight,
More potent as more heard,
As true as it's absurd."*
    Obama/Osama: *Nicholas Gordon*

53

Allah, my Allah

Allah, my Allah
Where are you?
I've come, all the way
To your home-'Kaaba' –
'Khana-e-Kaaba'
'Mere Allah ka Ghar---
Home of my God!

Storming wind plays with sands
Blowing and sweeping:
When acacia shrubs
Swayed in the desiccated hot breeze
Didn't I pay attention to you whispering?
"Don't cry, my child; don't try dying of tears"
"How can you say so, my Allah?
When I had so much of pain in the heart?
You beckoned my dear ones in this world
Why Allah, Why did you do it to me?"

"Cry not, my child,
You're close to me

You're mine,
A spark of the flame,
A reflection of me
Near to my heart, dear to my soul,
Stop, please stop sobbing,
I'm here to wipe your tears!"

2

Twinkling stars lighted up
His sky home was illuminated
Glittering lamps gazed down
Showering down blissful blessings

Seeing the full moon smiling
Cruising across the sky
I moved across the Arabian Desert
Searching for the holy nectar
To quench my anguished soul

I've reached your home
To see you, my Allah
Merging in the ocean of humanity
In the ocean of luminosity
I want you to cure my aching heart
Bless me Allah, by your magical touch
Deep, bleeding, wounds of my spirit
Allah, my Allah, where're you?

Sky cascaded pearly jewels
Rained down celestial waters
A Niagara of brilliance showering down
From the heaven above
Inundating Kaaba, the abode of Allah
Bridging with the heavenly abode
Holy Kaaba, my Allah Ka Ghar
To the sky dome—the sky home of my Allah!
Allah! My Allah! Where are you?
Aren't you there in your heavenly abode?

3

In the glistening moonlight
The plains of Arafat
At Masjid al-Haram Mosque
Draped in **Ihram**
White un-hemmed two sheets of cloth
Kissed the black stone of Kaaba
I joined the praying humanity
Circumambulating Kaaba
Seven times anticlockwise
Performing the holy Tawaf praying!

"***Bismillah***
Allahu Akbar! Allahu Akbar! Allahu Akbar!
Wa lil Lahi Ahmad!"
"*In the name of God,*

God is great! God is great! God is great!
And praise to be to God!"

"I'm like Abraham
You asked him to leave Hagar, his wife
Asked him to sacrifice his son Ishmael
I've to drink waters from the Well of Zam Zam
From that Holy Well, Angel Gabriel dug
Scraping sand with tip of his wing
Where water sprang gushing through thirsty sand!

I went to Mina, at the Mount Arafat
The Hill of forgiveness
Performed **Ramy al-Jamarat**
The Stoning of the Devil
Praying to thee, thy name, slept not
Whole night spent in thy prayers
Performed Eid al-Adha
The ritual of animal sacrifice too

Didn't I perform Tawaf again at Kaaba
In the undulating waves of humanity
In the light of moving white waves
I'm looking for you Allah, praying
I want your blessings!
Allah, my Allah, where are you?

I want to see you now
Your pearly smile
I want to feel you, now
Your divine touch
I want to listen to you, now
Your soothing words
And inhale your divine fragrance
To my lungs full—the musk of Eden
Allah, my Allah; now where are you?

You say, you're in every cell of me
Your splendour, thy divine energy
Let the power of your invisible
Invincible love flow through me
Let it be pumped through my blood
Let it be throbbing in my pulse beats
Let it, let it, my Allah
Let it breathe in and out of me!
I want always you in me
In every tick that ticks in my heart
Till it is done
All the ticks of the clock
That you presented at birth

"Labbaek, Allahumma Labbaek.
Labbaek, la shrike laka, Labbaeka.

Inna hamda wa nemata
laka wal mukkala sharika laka"
"Oh, Allah, here I am.
Here I am in thy presence.
Thou hast no equal. Here I am.
All praise for thee
And from thee are blessings.
To thee belongs all power
And rule though art without parallel."

Heaven showered light like flowers
In the splendour of the divine bliss
I beseech you, let me be forgiven
Forgive me, Hamzah

Didn't I hear my Allah's whisper from me;
"All mysteries of the world
Are absorbed in you
Your Allah, sent you Al-Quran
Your Hajj is over, now you're a Hajji!

Look inwards, begin again, a new search for me
Look deep, deeper and still deeper
In you, till you find me:
I'm there, in you
In the holy Kaaba of your heart
Like an invisible bird, nested in your soul

There I am tweeting
I'm there for you, and with you, forever!"
I do things for some reasons,
Which I cannot tell you now,
But you'll know, when the time is ripe,
There's a cause and a reason
For everything, I did
And all was done for a purpose!

A few Reflections:

"Whoever loves to meet Allah, Allah loves to meet him."

Prophet Muhammad

"The best richness is the richness of the soul."

Prophet Muhammad

"It is Allah who gives life and causes death, and Allah is seeing what you do."

Al Quran

54

Kalki's War Against the Antichrist

The Antichrist dived into the western ocean
Hunting for the Sun in his resting place
Abducted the Sun from his abode
And hammered down
Crucifying like a blazing painting in a fire frame
On the forehead of resting Night Mistress!

Powerless to be in motion any longer
Crippled in the horizon of freedom
Unable to breathe life any more
Counting down the last moments
The Sun blew the last flames in the air
Engulfing the Solar system
Together with his lovers
Earth, Moon and Planets in one go!

The Apocalypse began
Began the war of the Armageddon:

Note: Kalki is the 10th Avatar of Vishnu (Krishna), the Hindu God is used as a metaphor for the saviour of humanity in any crisis. The Antichrist is used as a metaphor for all the evil forces turning against humanity from time to time.

The Antichrist continued his nuclear dance,
Feeding bombs into the hungry mouths,
Having his last laugh of fury,
Exhibiting his ferocious, bloody canine teeth!
The final refuge of the universe—
The cause of all causes—
The soul of all souls—
The supreme consciousness of the cosmos—
The God who loves smiling
Lying on a coiled serpent bed
Over the waves of the Ocean of Milk
The 'Supreme Personality of Godhead'
Incarnated in time, as promised
In his mystic opulence in luminescence!

The God of the Future is ever in bliss
All incantations of gods rolled into one
Believes in coming and going
When evils mount up
Blazed inferno beyond the infinite spiralling galaxy
In a lightning, thundery, divine laughter
Parading the past, the present and the future
In his mysterious mind like cosmos
In the cosmic cave mouth of the universe
In his inherent effulgence
KALKI swallowed the Antichrist in a guzzle
Terminating evils consuming the universe
And saved goodness from extermination!

2

The countdown has already begun
For the Dark Age—KALI YUGA to end
It has reached the peak of the mountain,
Of accumulated sins of injustice
KALKI rushes to Shambala valley
Riding his swiftest white stallion
As the saviour of humanity,
Followed by the enthused liberated people
Isn't it time for KALKI to create a new world
Signifying the beginning
Of a new Age of Truth—
SATYA YUGA!

Out of sediments, the leader of the future will arise
From the mythical realm of Shambala
The leader of the future should arise
Like a comet wielding powerful weapon of compassion
To vanquish the evil barbarians of cruelty
As the leader of the whole universe
Riding on the swiftest white horse of a bright star idea!
Who's that unknown leader of the humanity -
The ultimate hope of the mankind?
Hasn't he taken birth by now in the world?
Where is the mythical realm – Shambala?
The mysterious place where the leader of humanity
Is anxiously waiting for God KALKI to bless him?

3

Kalki finds the Man of Future, lying starkly naked
Like the stone age cave man
In the cup-like valley of Shambala
Surrounded by pine tree-crowned green mountains
The Man of Future is drenched fully
In the pool of energy from the early morning sun
He curled like an embryo helplessly
On the Green Park meadow-bed
By the placid lake, far beyond the domes and towers
Having a mind full of nothingness
Emptied of ego, selfishness, envy and hypocrisy
To be filled anew with energy, hope and compassion -
A vision for the present and the future!

After the mighty war of the light and the darkness
The Man of Future is now at a loss
Thinking about whom he'll revolve, for;
He has witnessed the star-idea around he craves to rotate
Has been swallowed by a hungry, monstrous Black Hole
And he doesn't know how to recover the star-idea
From the cave mouth of the omnipresent Cloud-computing air
Kalki blesses the glorious smile that salutes the rising sun
Gratefully seeking for fresh energy to enrich the globe!

The monkey-infested Corridors of Power
Are finally liberated in the war for the good
The Summit Hill of Power remains now with the people
The files that deal with the human future
Are found bundled up in red tapes in a corner
Stinking terribly, being wrapped up, coated with heaps of thoughts
Of senile, ancient monkey-brain-droppings
The young, fresh air of freedom composes new melodious music
And stages there a new opera of exuberance to be played all over
The people make bonfire of the antediluvian files, singing and dancing!

Kalki rapidly vanishes in a moment into thin air amidst the people
Enters the hollow mind of the Bamboo Man of the Future
Occupies his evacuated mind with embryonic enthusiasm
And builds there the most sacred Temple of Hope
And at the sanctum sanctorum of the temple
Kalki lights the sacred Candle of Hope -
A Vision for the Future for the mankind
And meditates on a novel idea
Blazing at the heart of the Man of Future now

To be shared by all alive on Planet Earth in a split second on Facebook
Lighting billions of Candles of Hope at the altar of their hearts too!

The Man of Future gives a bountiful smile to the Rising Sun
And turns to the people gathered and beseeches;
"I'm humbled by your energy;
I'm now fully ready for the Song of Mahamudra
Are you ready for the new song, my dearest comrades?"
Crowd thundered in unison;
"Yes, we're ready, our Man of Future!
You're our Philosopher King
Take us ahead; lead us to make a new world for us!"
The Man of Future appeals to the people;
"Let us pour more colours on the canavas
Of the face of the future of mankind
Let us initiate painting a new symphony of bliss
Let us recreate the Golden Age in the Global Village
And build the Paradise we lost -
A biosphere of peaceful synchronicity -
An equitable, just, orderly, ecosphere -
A globe, not so warm, not weeping in melting glaciers,
But cool, natural and humane
To enjoy by all an elevated, joyful, copiousness!

A few Reflections:

"But the day of the Lord will come like a thief, and then the heavens will pass away with a roar, and the heavenly bodies will be burned up and dissolved, and the earth and everything done in it will be laid bare."

The Second Coming of Jesus: *Peter 3:10*

"Whenever there is withering of the law and an uprising of lawlessness on all sides, then I manifest Myself. For the salvation of the righteous and the destruction of such as do evil , for the firm establishing of the Law, I come to birth, age after age. (Bhagavad Gita, Book IV, Sutra.5.7.8)

Bhagavad Gita

"The whole world is divided for me into two parts; one is she, and there is all happiness, hope, light; the other is where she is not, and there is dejection and darkness..."

War and Peace: *Leo Tolstoy*

"And with tears of blood he cleansed the hand,
The hand that held the steel;
For only blood can wipe out blood,
And only tears can heal.

The Ballad of Reading Gaol: *Oscar Wilde*

"Let us do something, while we have the chance! It is not every day what we are needed. Not indeed that we personally are needed. Others would meet the case equally well, if not better. To all mankind they were addressed, those cries for help still ringing in our ears! But at this place, at this moment of time, all mankind is us, whether we like it or not. Let us make the most of it, before it is too late!
                           Waiting for Godot: Samuel Beckett

"And all shall be well
And all manner of things shall be well.
When the tongues of flame are in-folded
Into the crowned knot of fire,
And the fire and rose are one."
                              Four Quartets: T. S. Eliot

"The unleashed power of atom has changed everything save our modes of thinking, and thus we drift towards unparalleled catastrophe."
                                       Albert Einstein

"Let us remember that we can do these things not just because of wealth or power, but because of who we are: one nation, under God, indivisible, with liberty and justice for all.
                                       Barrack Obama

"The essence of warrior-ship, or the essence of human bravery, is refusing to give up on anyone or anything."
The Sacred Path of the Warrior: Chogyam Trungpa

"A leader is best when people barely know that he exists, not so good when people obey and acclaim him, worst when they despise him."
"Doing nothing is better than busy doing nothing."
Lao Tzu

"Every deed has its outcome. There's no escape from what we do. I enjoy the supreme treasure and joy, due to my virtue."
Jainism: Uttaradhyayana Sutra 13:10

"The trouble with the world is that the stupid are cocksure and the intelligent are full of doubt."
Bertrand Russell

"Democracy is a device that ensures we shall be governed no better than we deserve."
George Bernard Shaw

"To the man who only has a hammer, everything he encounters begins to look like a nail."
Abraham Maslow

> "Let us always meet each other with smile, for the smile is the beginning of love."
>
> **Mother Teresa**

> "All we are saying is: Give peace a chance."
>
> **John Lennon**

> "Blessed are peacemakers, for they will be called the children of God."
>
> **The Bible: *Matthew* 5.9**

> "The true and solid peace of nations consists not in equality of arms, but in mutual trust alone."
>
> **Pope John XXIII**

> "Yes I am, I am also a Muslim, a Christian, a Buddhist, and a Jew."
>
> **Mahatma Gandhi**

> "God did not create evil. Just as darkness is the absence of light, evil is the absence of God."
>
> **Albert Einstein**

Whispering Mind
K. P. Shashidharan

Whispering Mind is the love story of Yin and Yang, the negative and positive vibes in the world. They are eternal lovers like Shakti and Shiva; Prakriti and Purusha; Radha and Krishna; Adam and Eve. Representing the female and male energy forms in the universe, they circumambulate the cosmos in the speed of mind, a medium faster than electromagnetic waves.

Yin and Yang represent man and woman, lovers, life partners, friends, and in the Whispering Mind, Yin appears as Babe and Yang as Darling.

The romanticism of the poetry begins with their honeymoon in their journey of life and culminates in awareness, self-actualisation and infinite bliss. They live, love and pray; speak, act, sing, dance; eat, drink, travel; play and enjoy life; together, separate, united and departed; appearing, departing and reappearing. Their River of Life flows meandering through the panoramic landscape of the fifty-four poems in the book. Their interactions, joy of living, pathos, reflections on life, sunrise, sunset and moonlit nights of romance compose the poetry.

Whispering Mind is intended to induce joy in the mind, heart and soul with absorbing fables on life, love and bliss, spreading fragrance of blossoming flowers, stimulating the appetite of both traditional prose and poetry lovers. There is a wide variety of cuisine catering to the palate of gourmet.

Let us Enjoy Whispers of Our Mind!

Love the Moments!

Live in Them!

Celebrate Life and Its Moments!

Enjoy Reading! - 'Amuse Le Lecture!'